"I've been waiting for Terry to write this book ever since I first heard him talk about it. It's overdue! It's a must-read for every leader. I will highly recommend it to anyone who desires to be a healthy leader."

Doug Fields, veteran youth pastor, bestselling author, cofounder, downloadyouthministry.com

"Terry Linhart has given a gift to those of us who care about developing faithful leadership for the decades ahead. *The Self-Aware Leader* provides wonderful content and profound questions for reflection that can help leaders do the important inner work that is absolutely vital for long-term effectiveness in ministry. This is a wonderful resource, both for leaders and their mentors!"

Ken Knipp, VP of training, Young Life

"Grounded in years of experience in leadership development and a passion for seeing leaders flourish, Linhart brings much-needed attention to common blind spots that often hinder young leaders and provides biblical practices to address them. A must-read practical guide for leadership teams or anyone hoping to grow their effectiveness in leadership!"

Tom Lin, president/CEO of InterVarsity Christian Fellowship

"A few ministry leadership tours of duty convinced me that too many otherwise gifted people hit ineffectiveness walls because they were unable (or unwilling) to carefully consider the cracks in their foundations. As Terry Linhart points out, we've all got them. But when we're deluded into thinking that it's more important to give others what we think they want than to give them what we know we can offer, the temptation to 'act the part' gains a foothold in our hearts. This book is written by a friend who has become comfortable in his own skin and wonderfully fruitful as a leader, in part because he is fully committed to staying on the same journey he so carefully describes as necessary for the authentic, self-aware leader."

Dave Rahn, senior ministry advisor, Youth for Christ USA

"When I went into full-time ministry at twenty years old, I wish I'd had this book at my disposal. *The Self-Aware Leader* is an incredible tool for both individuals and teams, but it's especially helpful for young leaders learning to navigate ministry, leadership, and their own limitations for the first time. In this book, Terry helps leaders have the tough conversations necessary for growing in both self-awareness and Christlikeness."

Elle Campbell, author, speaker, cofounder of Stuff You Can Use

"This book is designed to equip young Christians to grow in their capabilities, devotion, and development and to maximize the vapor that God has given to each of us for his glory!"

John H. Sather, national director, Cru Inner City

"Fresh and relevant! This book brilliantly offers great insights and will challenge you to take a deeper look at how ministry has been done in the past. It is a game-changer for Christian youth workers desperately trying to stay in step with our rapidly shifting culture, providing real-life strategies for success! Bravo!"

Joan McClendon, project director, Women Entrepreneurship Initiative, Saint Mary's College

"In a society where people remain silent from having the conversations needed for healthy settings, ministries have relaxed and adopted the normalcy of allowing gaps among leaders. The young adult leader occupies the past and the present but is unable to lead well without addressing the day-to-day issues. My friend Terry provides practical exercises that will help organizations learn how to gather together, address issues, and adopt best practices to keep the lines of communication open and ongoing."

Fred Oduyoye, director of networking, Youth Specialties

"For years, Terry has helped equip young leaders like myself to serve the church well as pastors, ministry directors, missionaries, and more. The idea of learning to see in community what you cannot see on your own has been a constant thread in his work. The church is better because of leaders like Terry. In this project, *The Self-Aware Leader*, Terry stays true to form and offers piercing yet practical insight for rookie and seasoned leaders alike. While many leadership books can devolve into the realm of self-help, this work challenges us to overcome our blind spots by engaging in the critical, Spirit-led process of self-examination and communal reflection that moves a leader toward a place of confession, forgiveness, and growth. If you can only read one book on leadership this year, you should make it *The Self-Aware Leader!*"

Edrin C. Williams, The Sanctuary Covenant Church

"Terry Linhart has delivered a winning exploration of what you need to know about your past, present, and future leadership journey. Those you lead will thank you for reading this book."

Kara Powell, executive director of the Fuller Youth Institute, coauthor of *Growing Young*

"Terry takes us on a deep dive into the inner life of a leader, which truly guides all of life and leadership. He is gentle and gracious, yet direct and relentless, to go after the critical areas of a leader's life. If you allow it, this book will be a deep dive into your soul and character that will utterly transform your whole life."

April L. Diaz, author and speaker, Slingshot Group associate, director of coaching, The Youth Cartel

THE SELF--AWARE LEADER

DISCOVERING YOUR
BLIND SPOTS TO REACH
YOUR MINISTRY
POTENTIAL

TERRY LINHART

Foreword by Carey Nieuwhof

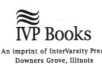

IVP Books

An imprint of InterVarsity Press
Downers Grove, Illinois

InterVarsity Press
P.O. Box 1400, Downers Grove, IL 60515-1426
ivpress.com
email@ivpress.com

InterVarsity Press® is the book-publishing division of InterVarsity Christian Fellowship/USA®, a movement of students and faculty active on campus at hundreds of universities, colleges, and schools of nursing in the United States of America, and a member movement of the International Fellowship of Evangelical Students. For information about local and regional activities, visit intervarsity.org.

All Scripture quotations, unless otherwise indicated, are taken from THE HOLY BIBLE, NEW INTERNATIONAL VERSION®, NIV® Copyright © 1973, 1978, 1984, 2011 by Biblica, Inc.™ Used by permission. All rights reserved worldwide.

While any stories in this book are true, some names and identifying information may have been changed to protect the privacy of individuals.

Cover design: Cindy Kiple
Interior design: Jeanna Wiggins
Images: © Rüstem GÜRLER/iStockphoto

ISBN 978-0-8308-4480-7 (print)
ISBN 978-0-8308-8106-2 (digital)

Printed in the United States of America ♾

Library of Congress Cataloging-in-Publication Data

Names: Linhart, Terry, 1964- author.
Title: The self-aware leader : discovering your blind spots to reach your
  ministry potential / Terry Linhart.
Description: Downers Grove : InterVarsity Press, 2017. | Includes
  bibliographical references.
Identifiers: LCCN 2016046958 (print) | LCCN 2016052036 (ebook) | ISBN
  9780830844807 (pbk. : alk. paper) | ISBN 9780830881062 (eBook)
Subjects: LCSH: Christian leadership. | Self-consciousness
  (Awareness)--Religious aspects--Christianity.
Classification: LCC BV652.1 .L573 2017 (print) | LCC BV652.1 (ebook) | DDC
  253--dc23
LC record available at https://lccn.loc.gov/2016046958

P   21   20   19   18   17   16   15   14   13   12   11   10   9   8   7   6   5   4

Y   34   33   32   31   30   29   28   27   26   25   24   23   22   21   20   19   18

TO JAY HOWVER

For your little nudge out the door and

this unexpected writing adventure

A PRAYER

*O Lord, who else or what else can I desire but you?
You are my Lord, Lord of my heart, mind, and soul. You know me
through and through. . . . Why, then, do I keep expecting happiness
and satisfaction outside of you? Why do I keep relating to you as one of
my many relationships, instead of my only relationship, in which all
other ones are grounded? Why do I keep looking for popularity,
respect from others, success, acclaim, and sensual pleasures?*

*Help me, O Lord, to let my old self die, to let die the thousand big
and small ways in which I am still building up my false self and trying to
cling to my false desires. Let me be reborn in you and see through
you the world in the right way, so that all my actions, words,
and thought can become a hymn of praise to you.*

*I need your loving grace to travel on this hard road that leads to
the death of my old self and to a new life in and for you. Amen.*

Henri J. M. Nouwen, *A Cry for Mercy:
Prayers from the Genesee*

*Nearly all wisdom we possess, that is to say, true and sound wisdom,
consists of two parts: the knowledge of God and of ourselves.*

John Calvin, *Institutes of the Christian Religion*

*We put no stumbling block in anyone's path,
so that our ministry will not be discredited.*

The Apostle Paul, 2 Corinthians 6:3

CONTENTS

CAREY
NIEUWHOF

I'm so thankful Terry Linhart wrote this book.
The journey he takes leaders on is so important.
Who doesn't want to keep their family together? Who
doesn't want to thrive and grow in their calling or be
more present for their kids? Terry shows us how we can
do all of these things and more when we are intentional
about staying aware of what we do and why we do it.

Almost everyone understands, at a superficial
level, that self-awareness is the key to so much. We
have Daniel Goleman's *Emotional Intelligence* to
thank for that. But we're left asking, *What does that
actually mean? What is self-awareness? And how would
I know if it's something I possess?*

That's where Terry's wisdom in this book will help.

I was moved into the world of self-awareness
somewhat involuntarily. When I was in my late
thirties, my wife told me it was time to get counseling.
I resisted. I was a pastor, after all—I sent people to
counseling. I didn't go to counseling.

Besides, the things she saw me doing that she
didn't like were also the same things that, in my
mind, made me "successful" in ministry. I couldn't

understand how my peers could recognize me for my achievements but the same recognition wasn't happening at home.

Here's the truth, though.

My wife was right.

I was dead wrong.

I now know that, at the time, what I lacked was any real self-awareness. My first walk into a counselor's office was some of the most difficult steps I have ever taken. As painful as the ensuing journey was, though, it was life saving. God was in the middle of it.

Much to my surprise, the healing (which initially feels like pain, by the way) didn't take away the things that made me effective; instead, it made me a very different (and better) person and leader.

I have a far better marriage. I'm a much better dad. I'm a better friend. And I lead with far more sensitivity, grace, and effectiveness than I ever did before.

My guess is some of you will love reading this book, and some of you will loathe it (even though it's really well written).

Before my trip to the counselor's office, I would have blown off a book like this. I would have thought it was for other people, or would have cherry-picked passages that made me think well of myself, or would have handed it to a friend. Today, it resonates and makes me so thankful books like this exist.

I would encourage you to read this book prayerfully and expectantly.

Socrates famously said that the unexamined life is not worth living. Solomon told us to guard our heart above all else, for from it flows the wellspring of life (Prov 4:23). They were both so right.

I hope you come to value this book. Sure, it will be a mirror. And only the brave look in the mirror. But the mirror you're holding will eventually morph into a window, a window into a redeemed future.

It's my prayer this book becomes both a mirror and a window for you.

PART OF MY JOB AS A PARENT was to serve as the initial driving instructor for each of my three teenagers. Though my hands occasionally braced against the dashboard, and my feet sometimes searched for a nonexistent brake pedal on my side of the car, we made it through the first days of driving on the road without incident. Topics for the first days of driving school with Dad: turn signals ("No you can't turn left from the right lane"), braking ("You don't use the accelerator when turning"), and explaining that being up on two tires during a turn was probably not a good thing.

As part of the lesson I showed them what they *couldn't* see. I demonstrated the reality of blind spots. After parking, I'd get out to stand along the left side of the car and ask them if they could see me in the mirrors. I was close enough that they could hear me talk, but as they looked in the mirrors, I wasn't visible. I explained how to "clear" their blind spots with a quick look over either shoulder. The intentional glance helped them see what they couldn't notice by looking ahead or at their mirrors. The glance let them see what was otherwise hidden, in this case a nervous father. I explained that when driving, there are often vehicles in their blind spots that pose a significant danger, and drivers can't see that without intentionally clearing the blind spot. I added that assuming things are safe without taking a careful look can be dangerous.

The phrase *blind spots* is regularly used in leadership circles to describe problems or patterns that lurk unseen and pose potential danger. For the last two decades I have been developing and equipping young adults to serve as ministry leaders, pastors, youth workers, missionaries, and managers. That process includes helping them reflect on what they may not notice, the areas of their life too personal or hidden to see easily, that may pose potential problems. The truth is that we all have such areas, even if we're not that young.

Over the years I've also noticed that few Christian organizations or churches help young leaders systematically and intentionally with their personal development. Most have an initial training program, but after that there is little ongoing support. As leadership presents increasing challenges and presses us, personal development is left up to each person and supervisors are sometimes at a loss how to step in and help. To their credit, it is difficult to bring up touchy matters when the issues are personal. It's easy to hope that time will fix areas where we're struggling, but it usually doesn't. If the problems persist, even with no help, sometimes a decision is made to make a change and try again with someone else. This inability to know what to do and how to help is contributing to some of the problems.

Recent national headlines have featured the departures of two well-known leaders of Christian organizations due to personal and moral issues. They were once seen as models of how to lead in ministries. In the last few months three friends of mine were released from their positions for difficult personal reasons. Despite the books, seminars, and articles about Christian leadership and the reminders to "lead ourselves first," problems persist. National ministry consultant Mark DeVries says that despite the glut of books and seminars, Christian leaders are still experiencing the same personal problems that previous generations of Christian workers have.[1]

The good news is that God is in the mending business. We weren't meant to be fragmented and disordered; we were meant to be whole—healed from our wounds by the saving power of Jesus Christ and open to the leading of the Holy Spirit. God can use cracked pots to carry valuable treasure (2 Cor 4:7). But unless we're intentional, *no one will talk to us about these blind spots*, these areas where we are inconsistent with the Spirit of Christ and his ministry. They're difficult to discuss. It might be difficult to talk to us about them too. Most of us think we're doing fairly well, but it's likely that the people we lead and work with would like us to grow in helpful directions. That's the reason I wrote this book.

One more thought before we move on: some may not be sure if being *self-aware* is a Christian practice, that it elevates self over Jesus. John Calvin wrote, "Nearly all wisdom we possess, that is to say, true and sound wisdom, consists of two parts: the knowledge of God and of ourselves."[2] We should be vigilant toward areas where our actions are incongruent with our message and faith. Otherwise we live a hypocritical life, uninterested in connecting with the Spirit of Christ (Jn 15) or unity with one another (Jn 17). Worse, we may even let areas of disobedience persist while being engaged in ministry. Timothy Keller commented, "If I am in denial about my own weaknesses and sin, there will be a concomitant blindness to the greatness and glory of God."[3]

Perhaps, then, it's more self-centered to *not* engage in self-awareness. Perhaps self-protection drives our aversion to this practice. Or maybe it's fear of what we may discover. We need to hear again the voice of love and grace from Jesus as he invites us to trust him and let him shepherd us as our Lord.

It's my desire that we grow in our intimacy with and knowledge of Jesus Christ, that our character increasingly reflects his, and that we engage in our ministerial work with greater effectiveness for God's glory. The goal is not to elevate self but to engage in biblical practices to discover places where we need God to forgive us, to infuse us with holiness and power, and to propel us forward in greater faithfulness and effectiveness in Christlike ministry with others.

MY STORY

In my mid-twenties I served in an urban ministry developing a Christian group in a racially divided community. I became the regional training coordinator for our three-state region and then the national trainer, teaching new Christian workers from across North America on the campus-oriented methodology and its values. I was taking on new leadership and teaching responsibilities within the organization. I loved the ministry I was called to, thinking I could be involved for my entire life.

All seemed to be going well until I went out to lunch with my executive director and learned that I was being let go. Though the reasons were unclear, my supervisor made a few comments about "fit" and "people problems." I couldn't hear the details because of the shock wave.

And that was it. I was done.

My leadership footing was pulled out by a rip current I hadn't noticed, and I was dragged out to emotional waters far over my head. I was swimming in shock, flailing to stay above waves of panic about what was next. Stunned and certainly embarrassed, I didn't know what to say to my supervisor or anyone else. I don't think I spoke much to anyone the rest of the day.

Though a variety of external factors contributed to my dismissal, the process exposed some problematic personal patterns I couldn't see. They had been an issue for years, but I was too busy, forward driven, and self-confident to notice. Now it seemed as if a stack of overstuffed baggage from my past had suddenly burst open, and I stared at a well-worn spiritual, emotional, and social mess.

Some of the issues I recognized; others, like veiled anger and a competitive spirit, seemed alien. They grew more evident to me once I started to reflect on my recent life. I remembered a scene from a few weeks before my dismissal when I had exploded in anger on a basketball court with mostly unchurched high school students. I was mad at and loudly arguing with the very young men I wanted to share the love and grace of Christ with. Of course they hadn't been calling fouls the right way, but what was worse is that I was oblivious to my actions and emotions, and completely missed what they were signaling about me.

Though I loved Jesus, I didn't know how to relate well to his people.

I had a choice to make: Do I prayerfully deal with my issues head-on or quickly gather everything together before someone noticed, turn on more charm, and move along? Should I acknowledge that I needed help or continue as though the problems were just "things I didn't do very well"?

Thanks to wise counsel, I chose to lean into the pain and face what I was discovering. God took my wife, Kelly, and me through a period of personal grief, pain, and a variety of temptations. It was a difficult but rich process marked with deep lows and triumphant small steps forward. That process was both a tailspin and a launching pad. Funny how that happens sometimes; what we see as crushing, God uses to reignite us. Though it was a difficult two years, we wouldn't trade that purifying wilderness time for anything. While we were numbed, scared, and scarred, it was the refining fire that God used to burn the dross from our lives and revealed (we're still trying!) two moldable people more ready for his imprint, direction, and grace. I needed to let the Holy Spirit continue to shape me and mold me, to address some issues of anger, pride, and even laziness that I couldn't see but were affecting my work and life. I needed to pay attention to my blind spots.

As I shared my story in seminars across the country, I consistently encountered young Christian leaders who were relieved that they weren't alone in facing private and personal difficulties. This is where the idea for this book was birthed, a book that would help those in Christian work grow and develop. I wanted supervisors, leaders of training programs, pastors, and office managers to have a resource that would help them with the personal development of their people in light of the tasks and demands of Christian ministry. Each chapter gives biblical examples and solutions for the problems and then provides practical and positive steps for moving forward in leadership growth. There are free resources for supervisors and small groups, and personal retreats are available on theselfawareleader.org.

DEVELOPING SELF-AWARENESS

In our early twenties we are still developing our identities in a period that theorists call "extended adolescence." We are still maturing while establishing our patterns and preferences. We are dealing with persistent temptations while being asked to step into significant shepherding roles as Christian leaders. And sometimes the personal demands on those of us in ministry are unattainable. See if the following job description sounds familiar:

We need someone young who is tirelessly hard-working, decisive, extroverted, funny upfront, able to mentor multiple people, and will send creative, handwritten notes to others (including staff!) on their important days. This person needs to possess a leadership style that attracts other volunteers in an instant, has proven executive savvy, and can instill vision and excitement with ease. He or she must handle conflict well, be strong yet humble, build a team with compassion, possess a gracious nurturing style, and be a self-starter. He or she must stay up with current trends and help promote the ministry through regular social media engagement, but always as approved by the oversight committee.

No one has the skill set to meet these expectations. Even if you could check off two or three, there would always be another expectation to keep you from feeling successful. It's difficult, sometimes impossible, to hide from the pressure to perform flawlessly in ministry, to not fail, and to not let others down. In reality our weaknesses, sin, and blind spots don't stay hidden for long under such scrutiny and pressure. They get pressed out for all to see.

The second reason blind spots exist is our capacity for self-deception. The classic bestseller *Leadership and Self-Deception* by the Arbinger Institute says, "There is nothing more common in organizations than self-deception."[4] The book went viral based on word-of-mouth recommendations because we all understand that the issues start with the deceptive ways we treat each other, especially at work (including ministries). As Gordon Smith defines them, self-discerning persons are "conscious of their own capacity for self-deception and thus of their vital need for the encouragement, support and wisdom of others."[5]

Smith says the same is true for Christians: "In humility we must recognize our capacity for self-deception, self-absorption, and self-gratification."[6] Our hearts can be deceptive. We can follow our passion, but they may not be the right passions. We can do what comes instinctively, but our instincts may seek self-protection (Jer 17:9). Any trained counselor can confirm that some older leaders have become quite skilled at deceiving themselves. Christian counselors could list the creative ways they've seen people excuse persistent sins. We have defense mechanisms that create narratives of excuses, blame, and accusations that move the responsibility for and reality of situations off ourselves. David Benner says we don't have to choose self-deception. It is, like a computer, the *default* story of our lives.[7]

This book comes from the ministry trenches where you and I work each week. It's not detached theory but practical reality from one who also works in messy ministry every week. In fact, this is a dangerous book to write because the illusion is then that I have it all together. In reality, though, I am still striving each week to be like Jesus in life and leadership and am working on my own blind spots and recognizing my need for God.

Not living authentically, where what we teach is supported by how we live, is a life of hypocrisy. Developing self-awareness is an honest examination of God's work, our limits, the Holy Spirit's gifting, our weakness, and of our work in ministry. It's embracing Jesus' discipleship call to deny ourselves, even die to self, and take up the cause of Christ for our lives (Lk 9:23). It involves times of confession as well as celebration and joy. It includes an embrace of who God has created us to be, that who we are is not a mistake or something less that the best of God's creative work. The apostle Paul modeled self-awareness, being conscious of the influence of the flesh (2 Cor 12:7-9; Gal 5:17), of his weaknesses (2 Cor 11:30), of his obedience (2 Tim 4:7), of his background and history (Phil 3:4-14), of his social interactions with others (1 Thess 2:6-8), and of his ministry (Rom 1:14-16).

I've written this to be an encouragement and to help your work be as fruitful as possible as you get to know God better. It's my ultimate hope that Jesus becomes dearer to you as you serve him, that you'll develop a close friendship with him, and that you see the Holy Spirit use you in ways you know you can't take credit for.

At the end of each chapter I've included some practical next steps for your personal or group reflection. If you visit theselfaware leader.org, you'll find free resources such as group activities, retreat guides, and resources for supervisors to help groups, classes, training programs, and supervisors interact with the topics of this book in helpful ways.

I consider it a privilege to walk with you through these few chapters, and I'm grateful to the many people who have contributed material, provided ideas and anecdotes, and have given editorial assistance along the way. I offer these chapters as my "loaves and fish," and pray that Christ will bless them and multiply them into a holy and effective work in your life and in the lives of those you lead for the glory of God.

1

I WAS THIRTEEN YEARS OLD and about to make a very painful choice. The high school coaches were recruiting middle school athletes for various sports. While the football coach described the gridiron possibilities as being akin to a military boot camp, the cross country coach took a different tack. He said that *smart* guys run cross country. My grades didn't reflect it, but I considered myself smart, so I signed up. That action undermined my self-assessment.

That first, hot August day, Coach started practice with a simple instruction: "Go out and run three for a warm-up and meet me on the track." I thought, *I can do this. Three laps around the track aren't bad!* At the end of what I breathlessly learned was three *miles* of warm-up, my body screamed for relief. *Who runs three miles to warm up? That is the run!* In agony, I jogged in far behind my teammates and overheard Coach calling the next level of suffering "interval training," a torturous series of quarter-mile sprints, with sixty seconds of rest in between. Thirty minutes later, we then ran 2.5 miles—just to cool down!

Smart people run cross country? Right.

I went home that night and spent some sick time in the bathroom. A few days later Coach called my dad and asked, "How is Terry enjoying cross country?" Dad, despite my body's rebellions, replied, "I think he likes it."

"Good!" Coach said, "I hope he hangs in there. He has a lot of potential."

Potential. I wasn't sure I could survive each evening, let alone run a similar practice the next day. And the next. For a whole season. I'm not sure what Coach's or Dad's opinions about my potential were based on; I couldn't see it. And I certainly didn't feel very smart by choosing that sport. In my first race I even set the school record for the *slowest* time in the history of my high school.

On the last day of practice, Coach asked the five of us who were freshmen to meet with him. "How good do you ninth-grade guys want to be?" he asked. "You could be a strong varsity team in the future. I see five guys here with a lot of potential." Coach even looked right at me when he said that last part. *Potential*—it made me feel good.

We looked around at each other and Andy blurted, "I want to win state."

"State! We want to win state!" we all said excitedly, adolescent voices cracking with youthful optimism. Being the best in our whole state was a big goal, but Coach nodded his approval. We got the message and left with "win state" as a common goal for our year-round running friendship.

That next autumn I found myself at the front of the pack in the junior varsity race. As our group came into view from behind the school building, everyone realized that Linhart was in first place, with a mile to go. I held the lead to the final turn and finished in first place. I was pumped—potential indeed!

From that point on, I never looked back. I saw my running and myself differently. And Coach knew that he could push me to new levels in practice and performance. By the end of that season I was the second fastest runner on the varsity team. For the next two years I walked to each starting line knowing that I had a shot to win that race.

The story differed for my "freshman five" teammates. One runner made poor lifestyle choices that hurt his training. Another broke his leg and never ran well after that. Another chose a different sport, while the fourth tired of practicing and his times slowed. During one race our senior year, as faster and younger runners lapped him, I heard him sarcastically say, "Hey buddy, win state." The very goal that we had once set became a bitter theme he used to mock others who wanted to succeed.

Most of us want to do our best in Christian ministry. We want God to use us effectively in working with others, and we want to be faithful in using the gifts and skills God has given us. We don't want to experience problems, fail, burn out, drop out, or mess up. Yet it happens. Too often. Despite our potential.

Usually without being able to see them, we develop habits and attitudes that give shape to our leadership and ministry. Tim Elmore calls these "habitudes" and says that leadership "runs 360-degrees. We influence others all around us. We must first lead ourselves."[1] We must lead ourselves before we lead anyone else. Yet, we don't naturally lead ourselves well. Despite our potential. Despite the many books on the topic.

But we could avoid many problems. We *could* lead ourselves well.

So, what happens?

When teacher and author Henri Nouwen reflected on his life in leadership, he noticed a level of dissatisfaction and unhappiness, prompting him to make some significant changes: "I found myself living poorly, living somewhat isolated from other people, and very much preoccupied with burning issues. Everyone was saying that I was doing really well, but something inside was telling me that my success was putting my own soul in danger."[2]

Nouwen's aha moment comes at the intersection between self, behavior, and the spiritual life. It's where we often lose our way, unknowingly turning life transformation into mere self-help, polishing the veneer on our lives to give the impression of something solid underneath. We emphasize our charm and personality while never letting our foot off the accelerator, as if more of everything will solve any weakness.

LACING UP FOR THE RUN

God isn't satisfied with skin-deep spirituality. He calls us to become transformed to the likeness of Christ inside and out, a work that only he can do. Paul and the writer of Hebrews explain the process using the image I started this chapter with, athletic training.

Paul was committed to helping people know the freedom in Christ through the gospel. But to share that freedom Paul talks about his hard work. He described self-examination and the resulting change in attitude and behavior as being like an athlete who trains in order to complete a race (1 Cor 9:24-27; Gal 2:2; 5:7; Phil 2:16; 2 Tim 4:7). And he says that if athletes train hard for a simple medal, people working with eternal matters should train even harder. "I discipline my body and keep it under control," Paul writes, so that he won't be disqualified from his ministry (1 Cor 9:27 ESV).

Paul's image challenges us to ask serious questions: What does pushing ourselves look like when it comes to ministry? I mean, how do we push ourselves to love others well? Does it mean that once a week we look for particularly difficult people and patiently spend time conversing with them? What is involved with pushing ourselves to faithfully reflect the love of Christ? The answers may be very different than those found in popular definitions for leadership success.

We find the image of running again in Hebrews. After describing those who were faithful to God, the writer puts us in a stadium. In chapter eleven the stands are filled with those who have already successfully completed their lives (and races), and then we're encouraged to "throw off everything that hinders and the sin that so easily entangles" so we can "run with perseverance the race marked out for us" (Heb 12:1). Believers are told to fix their "eyes on Jesus" (v. 2) and then work and train so that they can run the long race set before them: faithful obedience to God and ministry to others.

We understand getting rid of the sin that trips us up, and we'll talk more about those temptations and sins in chapter four, but what are we to "throw off"? Some commentators politely suggest the author is referring to the removal of weights that runners commonly used while training. However, the more accurate image comes from understanding running. You wear extra clothing to stay warm, to stay dry, to stay modest. When you get to the line, all of that goes because you want to run lightly. In first-century competitive running, this included stripping off all clothes. The runners were completely naked so they wouldn't be slowed by anything that could keep them from running their best race, nothing that would allow others to pull them back. Focusing on Jesus, the writer suggests, means following his example: abandoning our carefully cultivated images and our comfortable surroundings, and running unashamedly.

Paul used a similar image when he challenged Timothy to train himself to be godly (1 Tim 4:7). The Greek word for *train* is closely related to the word for *naked*. In the first gymnasiums where the Greeks trained for the Isthmus Games, the centerpiece of Corinthian sports, the athletes trained without any hindrance.[3] When we take the first steps toward becoming our authentic self, the process reveals our weaknesses, sin, vulnerabilities, and hindrances. Releasing our defensiveness and excuses can at times leave us feeling a bit naked. It's not fun when someone taps us on the shoulder and gently (or not) points out an instance when we didn't lead well or behaved poorly.

What does this training process look like? There's a good example in Paul's letter to the church in Colossae:

> You used to walk in these ways, in the life you once lived. But now you must also rid yourselves of all such things as these: anger, rage, malice, slander, and filthy language from your lips. Do not lie to each other, since you have taken off your old self with its practices and have put on the new self, which is being renewed in knowledge in the image of its Creator. (Col 3:7-10)

"Rid yourselves" means to take off or discard something, like worn-out clothing. The task is ours, not someone else's. Paul lists old practices (anger, rage, malice, slander, filthy language) that have no place in the Christian life, but were (and are) common among Christians.[4] Let's face it, ministry is a very human process. It's difficult to navigate the personalities, preferences, and self-centeredness that we each bring to our work together. Though we'll never be perfect (and there *will* be conflict), Paul never quit encouraging his readers to be faithful. We need to examine our habits and thinking so we can faithfully work with and lead others, choosing to run the race to win (1 Cor 9:24), and being willing to strip off that which hinders us.

It isn't enough to get rid of the old; we need to take that second step to put on the new self that God fashions in us. In the gym we are to put on new ways of living: "Compassion, kindness, humility, gentleness and patience" (Col 3:12). We are to build these into our heart and mind and actions, so that every heartbeat, every thought, every work of service has been practiced and purified. It becomes second nature to have our new nature guiding us. We can never settle or coast, but rather do the work necessary to be authentic—toward God, toward others, and toward ourselves.

The leadership gym is the proper place to talk about self-knowledge in light of ministry with others. Once we let down our self-protective defenses, we can work with the Holy Spirit to gain a clear picture of what is under our life layers. We can elicit the help of others to peer into areas of our life we can't easily see but may need attention. Parker Palmer notes that "self-care is never a selfish act—it is simply good stewardship of the only gift I have."[5]

DARING TO GLANCE

One helpful, practical tool to understand our blind spot is what's called the Johari Window, an image developed as a counseling tool in the 1950s.[6] Subjects were given a list of fifty-six adjectives, and were asked to pick those that best described them. The same was done with peers of each subject, and then all of the answers were placed on the grid for discussion.

There are four areas on the grid (see fig. 1). The areas that are known to us and to others are termed our *open* areas. Others do not know about some areas of our lives because they are *hidden*, but we know them well. And there are *unknown* areas that contain things we and others don't know about us. And then we have *blind spots.* These are the things we don't know, though they are clear to others.

	Known to Self	Not Known to Self
Known to Others	OPEN	BLIND SPOTS
Not Known to Others	HIDDEN	UNKNOWN

Figure 1. The Johari Window

The contents of our blind spots are not necessarily negative. We may have a gift or opportunity that we can't see but is plain to others. We may overlook some of our successes that others notice. For example, I was unaware that teaching was my spiritual gift until I taught at a national conference. After the first day, the two conference coordinators pulled me aside and suggested I may want to explore teaching as a future direction. I was so focused on another direction that I couldn't see how much of what I was drawn to and was doing was instructional in nature. And now, what a delight it is to do the same with other young leaders and help them recognize their gifting as they set out to lead in ministry settings.

BE AWARE

It may be helpful to clarify a few things at this point:

- The glance into blind spots is not a self-help pursuit, something we do to be a better "me." It's a time of discernment, a humble openness to the Holy Spirit's guidance, a process that often leads to confession, forgiveness, and new direction.

- The prayerful exploration of blind spots is best done within a supportive community to help us be thorough. This may be the most difficult aspect for us, and that may tell us something about ourselves and our situations.

- The exploration of blind spots is particularly necessary for driven and future-oriented people.

- Leadership's currents pull us toward a level of self-sufficiency where we don't seek anything that might make us uncomfortable or confront our confidence, to our own detriment, and even potentially to our demise.

LIVING LIKE WE LOVE

At the heart of all this talk about transformation is love. God's love for us. God's love through us for others. We aren't loved because of what we have done. While we were still sinners Christ died for us (Rom 5:8). We don't love because of what others have done for us. Love your enemies, Jesus said. Pray for those who persecute you (Mt 5:44). We are loved because that's who God is. We love because that's what God shows.

It doesn't matter what we want to do in ministry, the ultimate source of success is the Holy Spirit's activity in our hearts and in the hearts of others. Our trust in Christ, our motives, our convictions, and the source of our actions exist in our hearts. It's where our love for Christ and for others grows or is stifled. In my marriage, family, and work, I remind myself of how Jesus described love,

"Greater love has no one than this: to lay down one's life for one's friends" (Jn 15:13).

Paul is our model here. He had every right to rest on his authority, but he laid his life on the line repeatedly for one purpose: love. We don't often describe Paul as "loving." He certainly didn't seem like a touchy-feely guy in his writings. But maybe we have an incomplete picture. He said it plainly, "Christ's love compels us, because we are convinced that one died for all, and therefore all died. And he died for all, that those who live should no longer live for themselves but for him who died for them and was raised again" (2 Cor 5:14-15).

Christ's love compels us. We read that phrase too quickly and miss the implications. In spite of Paul's drive and focus on action, his motivation changed when he met Christ. The man who once uttered "murderous threats" (Acts 9:1) was transformed by Jesus and now speaks of the tender, brotherly affection he had for the church and that he wanted them to have for each other (Rom 12:10; Phil 1:8). Paul was now compelled by Jesus to love others rightly.

Living out God's love challenges everything. It means we no longer can live for ourselves. We can't live only for our relationship with Jesus, our own advancement, or in constant self-protection. As we work on our blind spots, our goal is not self-promotion; the goal is Christlikeness and greater reflection of his love to others. Love means we live to serve others—otherwise, we can't call it *love*, can we? It ends up being something else.

So, how are you doing at loving others in your workplace? Among your ministry team? Around your home? How would others answer those three questions about you?

Loving others is rooted in Jesus' love for us. When John tells the story of how Jesus washed the disciples' feet, he says, "Jesus knew that the hour had come. . . . Having loved his own who were in the world, he loved them to the end" (Jn 13:1). Then he picked up a towel and a basin of water and washed the feet of all the disciples, even Judas. He showed how leaders serve the people they lead, how they move through a room unseen, how they treat people who don't trust them. Jesus then explained that if they want to be fruitful, it will blossom from the roots of love, love first found in him (1 Jn 4:19). If the disciples didn't understand his loving service then, they certainly did days later when they reflected on his death and resurrection, what he chose to endure so that they and we can experience forgiveness and eternal life.

The foundational reason for examining our lives and blind spots is so we can be more like Christ in our work. Jesus made clear the connection between the loving presence of Christ and being fruitful in ministry. He commissioned the disciples to "go and bear fruit" (Jn 15:16-17), and reminded them to stay connected to the vine. This is where we often get it wrong. We think we can bear fruit without being closely connected to Christ, that our weaknesses don't matter, or that a "little sin" in our lives isn't that big of a deal. Instead of cultivating a love that has heavenly origin, we put on our "ministry face," use our gifts at our own discretion, and end up drawing people to ourselves instead of Jesus. That's like someone duct taping fruit to trees and calling it fruitful.[7]

Paul was *compelled* by love. We can read Paul's letters with an activist mindset, noting his drive and missional accomplishments. Others of us read Paul and see him like a middle school's vice principal who keeps us (the church) in line with sound doctrine and right behavior. What if we started to read his epistles with an eye on Christ's love, deep affection on a mission of grace and forgiveness? Love washes the meanness out of religion, meanness that even the Christian variety can be notorious for having.[8] Love compels us, and permits us, to look into our blind spots.

Arika was an outgoing and vibrant staff member able to coordinate ministry with a contagious enthusiasm. Other staff members loved working with her and felt confident in her work—as long as things were going well. But the moment that any words from other staff felt like criticism, she would immediately shrink back, hiding both her defensiveness and discouragement. Arika became silent, focused, and hyper-task-oriented, all masking the strange mix of pride and insecurity.

I noticed the change more than once and asked about it. I could tell she didn't even like my question. A few days later she shared that every time someone corrected her, she felt stupid and inadequate. I said that it wasn't just when people criticized her, but also when others offered her ideas that differed from hers. I asked Arika why it *felt* like they were condemning her. She paused and then said, "Every time that happens I can hear my high school math teacher when he said my homework was the worst he'd ever seen and added that I must be dumb. Here I am an adult in my early thirties, and I still can't shake those words out of my head."

I'd like to say that she was able to correct it. She didn't. Arika's self-protection got worse in the following years. As her three coleaders wanted to take the ministry in a different direction, she thought they didn't like her. In fact, she extended that opinion to other areas in the entire organization and eventually walked away, never to work with them again. She was unable to make the separation between issues about the ministry and a potential personal attack.

We all have been shaped by our interactions with others (we'll deal with that more thoroughly in chapter three), and we can recall encouraging and demeaning statements made about us in the past. Too many of us have had hurtful things said to us by teachers, parents, coaches, siblings, and friends that still haunt us. For Arika, an old wound festered into a lie that she believed, which eventually took her out of ministry for good. She's never volunteered anywhere since.

RACING WITH THE COACH

A few weeks after I won my first cross country race, I was involved in a large regional meet. I was running in fifth place at my best pace, feeling confident in our team and satisfied that I would finish in the top five among such a large group of runners. At a mid-race flag, I made the turn and dropped my eyes to the ground, watching my bright Nike Vainqueur racing spikes dig in and push me forward. As I did, I heard Coach Jones's voice, "OK, Linhart, if you don't catch that guy in front of you, we lose."

Coach was jogging alongside me, which didn't make me feel good about my pace. He then raised his voice and seemed upset, "You're too complacent here in fifth place. Come on, Linhart, you're capable of doing better. Dig down. It's time to show me what you've got. Get that fourth-place guy right now. You can do it. It's time." And he jogged away in irritation.

I had never heard Coach talk like that, especially to me. He attended my dad's church. *Hey, be nice; I'm the pastor's kid!* The coach who had been so kind in my early days and had even looked at me when he said that our team had a lot of potential was now challenging me to pick up my pace. Though I felt like I was running my best, and was doing great compared to the rest of my team, I picked my knees up higher and pumped my arms stronger with each stride. I set my eyes on the fourth-place runner and started to gain. With a half mile to go, I passed him and crossed the finish line in fourth. We won the race—by one point. As I exited the finish-line chute, Coach Jones's smile couldn't be contained as he ran up to hug me. "I knew you could do it," he said. "Great job."

That scene has flashed in my mind multiple times as I've finished these chapters. We are off and running in ministry. Some of us have been running for a while and others are just leaving the starting line. We set a pace, hit our stride, and start leading forward, grinding out the miles. The habits and attitudes of how we do ministry and interact with others have become familiar. We might be doing well, keeping up with others, certainly, and not lack for confidence, until the coach jogs up. We've been preoccupied with our steps, appearance, and pace, and his voice intrudes into our complacency, refocusing us on the reasons we're running in ministry.

What is the end goal for paying attention to our blind spots? It's not the attention. For runners, no one claps as they run the miles day after day preparing for the race. No crowds line the riverbanks for rowing crew practice. There are no grandstands along the walls of a weight room with fans cheering on the CrossFit folks. Photographers don't roam libraries to capture pictures of those studying in pursuit of a graduate degree while also working full-time jobs.

Discipline usually happens away from the spotlight. The end—the finish line, the final buzzer, or the commencement stage—is where it's recognized. The diligence in being better ministers and leaders also takes place where no one can see. The fruitfulness of our ministry, as measured by God's standards, is where we can recognize and judge the results, and sometimes not even then! When we cross the finish line and the race is over, we'll listen for those words, "Well done, good and faithful servant" (Mt 25:21). *I knew you could do it. Great job.*

With this book, I want to run alongside you and encourage you to run your best race. It is worth your best effort. If we want to be faithful and effective to what God has called us to, then we need to lift our heads, examine our strides, glance over our shoulders, and maybe even pick up the pace. I feel a coach-like urgency today, because too many people are experiencing personal problems in ministry leadership. Too many supervisors aren't sure how to address issues they see in those they lead. Too many ministries are engaged in petty arguments, some of them quite public, and people are walking away from churches and ministries for reasons without merit.

What if we set for ourselves the lofty goal to evidence the personal integrity, graciousness, and boldness that should characterize Christian leaders? Is that goal achievable? I would like to think so, or at least I think that we *should* want it to be a goal.

SELF-CHECK

So, what's our first move? We've all heard how valuable spiritual reflection is, but seriously, when was the last time we did it? Before you go too much farther in this book, it would be good to schedule a time to be alone with God. It's your first step in the race ahead. If you are able, remove the everyday items that fill your time—the technology, consumeristic patterns (no coffee shops, bookstores, or conferences), and information (sports and news outlets) that have become the routine. Be alone. Just you and God. Be open to the reality that God may want to do a fresh work in your life and ministry.

One of the important practices I've found helpful is to take retreats of various lengths on a regular basis. This difficult but necessary activity allows us to attend to God's voice in our life. When we're away, even if only for a few hours, we can identify what pushes for our attention. We develop a new awareness of the clues that our life might be trying to give to us about important matters.[a] We can't see the clues unless we're silent . . . still . . . humble . . . attentive . . . listening. In retreat, as we read and reflect on God's Word and enter into extended periods of prayer, we experience the fresh leading of the Holy Spirit.

At theselfawareleader.org, I have provided two short guides, one for a four-hour retreat and the other a two-day format, that are tools to help you develop a regular practice of extended reflection and prayer.

---

[a] Parker Palmer, *Let Your Life Speak: Listening for the Voice of Vocation* (San Francisco: Jossey-Bass, 2000).

If you're reading this book, then you're likely in a position where others have recognized your potential. They see that you can be used of God to have a significant effect on the lives of others and that your honest intention is to do well, the best that you can. The divine Coach is calling you to the starting line. You can see a little of the course ahead. He looks to you and asks, "How far do you want to go?" You look up, then out at the course ahead, turn, and reply with the equivalent of "I want to win state!" As your race begins, with a gleam in his eye, the Coach reminds, "I've created you, gifted you, loved you with my life. You have potential. Run your best!"

Leadership isn't one big race; it is a bunch of little races with little finish lines to cross along the way. The following chapters identify some of the common little races that we Christian ministry leaders face—practical matters that need attention if we want to be faithful to God's calling. Some chapters will seem amazingly relevant now, while others may be so in the future or not at all. Some chapters will take a level of honesty and self-awareness on your part that may be challenging. Some themes will require that a trusted friend or two join in on this run. If you're willing to press toward your potential, may you allow God to speak as you read, and may the Holy Spirit help you live out the truth in life and ministry.

You've got potential.

Run your *best*.

Let's start now.

FOR GREATER AWARENESS

1. If someone said to you that you have tremendous potential, what would be your first response? Would you agree, shrug your shoulders, disagree, or feel pressured? Why do you think that

would be your response? Do you *feel* like God thinks you have potential? Why or why not?

2. Look back on times when you discovered a blind spot in your life. How did you see in that situation? Why weren't you able to notice it before?

3. Do you think you relate well to others? How do you think *others* would describe your ability to relate well with them? What irritations have you noticed in you as you work in ministry situations? What do those irritations suggest about you?

4. Privately ask three people who know you well, "If you were my coach trying to help me perform at the highest levels of relational and emotional competency, what assessment would you give me in those areas? What exercises would you give me to improve?" Listen to them and write down what you hear.

5. Go to three people under your leadership and say, "I'm trying to learn what I don't yet know about myself in leadership. Tell me what you experience under my leadership—the stuff I might not know."

6. Before you continue in this book, write a four or five sentence prayer that could serve as your prayer of commitment for your time working through this book.

2

HUMANS ARE INCREDIBLY GIFTED AT SORTING. We
distinguish between colors, sounds, speeds, and
styles. Often this is wonderful, delightful, and life-
saving. At times it is devastating. Recently, some
friends described something I had done as special
and helpful to them. I was grateful to have helped
them in that way, but I look at the others they work
with and think, *Why am I being mentioned? I'm not as
self-sacrificing as those people.* In fact, as far as I know,
I'm not even as helpful as the friends who were
thanking me.

You see how destructive this thinking is? I mean,
a group of people I love describe me as helpful. I
react with, "Thank you, but I'm not that good."
Which is actually saying, "Thank you, but you lack
discernment." And I can spend so much energy on
the process of being humble that I don't go ahead
and do the work I am called to do.

I'm pretty sure that I'm not alone. I talk to many
people about life, and our conversations often take us to
the spiritual components of life. I find people constantly

comparing themselves to others, saying, "That person is really spiritual. I could never be that way."

My friend Jon Swanson has been looking at Bible characters used as bad examples.[1] We are told that we should not be as _____ as these people. For example, even people who don't know much about church stuff have heard about "doubting Thomas" (Jn 20:24-29). Martha always gets identified as the unspiritual of two sisters, the one who was too busy to spend time listening to Jesus (Lk 10:38-42).

What Jon has been realizing is that those people are normal people like us. Jesus didn't ignore them or write them off. He worked in their lives. And each of these people had opportunities to shine. In fact, the famous people may have spent some time saying, "I wish I could be as courageous as Thomas" after he suggested the disciples follow Jesus toward Jerusalem even though it could cost their lives (Jn 11:16). Or saying, "I wish I could be as faithful and hospitable as Martha" when she told Jesus she believed he was Messiah and later hosted a meal in honor of Lazarus and Jesus (Jn 11:17-43; 12:1-2).

We need God to use us, and not settle for comparisons for our direction and our fulfillment. And the first step is to see ourselves clearly.

BECOMING BOB LAURENT

The college I attended held an annual conference for high school students. One year our conference speaker was Bob Laurent. As he took the stage for the Friday chapel, I marveled at Bob's charisma, dynamic warmth, and palpable enthusiasm for his message. I hadn't watched any speaker display the kind of love for Christ and the gospel that Bob did. He was energetic, joyful, and clearly cared about his listeners. It didn't take long before that nineteen-year-old me decided he wanted to speak like Bob.

I bought an audio recording of his talk and played it repeatedly until I had it memorized. I learned each of Bob's stories and expressions. I even worked on saying his funny lines with the unusual voice he used for "Herbie," the boy in his story. The ironic part, lost on me at the time, was the main point of his talk, a challenge for us to "be real." I clearly missed the point.

A year later I was a guest speaker at an area high school event, and I gave that well-rehearsed talk. I tried Bob's jokes, told the humorous stories, used his funny voices, and waited. Crickets. The audience just sat there. The students barely laughed, and when they *did* chuckle, it looked like they were looking to each other to check if it really was funny or not. It evidently wasn't.

I couldn't understand it! I was doing everything *exactly* the way Bob did, but it wasn't working, and I began to panic. Not knowing how to fix it, I kept speaking while that little voice in my head started to condemn not only the talk but my potential effectiveness in ministry. The event seemed like a flop. I drove home that night feeling like a failure, wondering if I had what it takes to be in Christian ministry or speak in front of groups.

Many years later I interviewed for a ministry position and was quite nervous about its fit for Kelly and me. Unknown to me, Bob was part of that search committee. As the interview concluded, he walked me down to the building's front door. He commented to me, "I think that went really well." After some small talk, he shared some advice, "Don't try to be like someone else. What we need here is *you*. What these college students need is *you*, your unique gifts, and your *enthusiasm*. I'll tell you," he continued, "you're going to be tempted to be like the others here, but you give these students your best, and don't try to be anyone else."

His words caught me by surprise and I chuckle even now as I remember them. The man I once tried to mimic was telling me to face my insecurities and resist the desire to imitate. He knew firsthand that Christian leaders regularly face fear and insecurity. He understood that the imitation shortcut seems easier, but it cuts corners that are part of God's unique intentions for our lives.

SELF IN THE BLIND SPOT

I want to highlight some unhealthy elements of our self that may be hidden in our blind spots.

Dissatisfaction. It's easy to become dissatisfied with the gifts and skills that God has given to us. Instead of developing our own abilities, talents, and opportunities, we wish for someone else's. We look around and wish we were more like someone else. Even at this point in my ministry life, I face that temptation. (It's more common among veteran leaders than you know.)

One of my colleagues is easily one of the smartest people I've ever known. He dresses with style, never seems to say anything wrong, is a gifted musician, is a gracious listener, and every class he teaches seems flawless. To complete the package, whatever he writes is captivating in its depth, humor, and wisdom. Even fifteen years after Bob talked to me about not comparing myself to others in my work, it's too easy to watch my colleague and feel like I'm wearing velour sweatpants to the cool kids' prom.

Competing. We never escape the temptation to compete with others. It was a consistent problem for Jesus' disciples. We are tempted to establish our worth or value based on how we rank against others. Once we spot our competitive spirit and its roots in pride or insecurity, we can begin to discover why we desire to be ranked (usually only in our minds) ahead of others. That is the moment when our self-centered motivations are revealed and we need to confess them to God. Truly, we need to celebrate others' gifts and successes rather than be jealous or envious of them.

Insecurity. The issue that underlies the rest may be insecurity, which is not a new problem for Christian workers. Some cover their insecurities with a variety of masks: fear, conceit, anger, and withdrawal. Others work to authenticate themselves, to prove their worth and value via their accomplishments. Some use bullying to establish self-confidence or significance, excusing their behavior toward others as just their personality type. What all of these have in common is a gauge of success based on the approval or acceptance of others, the twin siblings of insecurity and the shadows of ego.

Please don't succumb to the cycle of self-despising and despair. You have been created with personality, body, mind, and soul uniquely your own, given by God. There is a dance only you can perform, one that you do not create alone but cultivate as you follow the Holy Spirit's leading. Don't mar the divine artistry at work within you.

PASSING THE SMELL TEST

Søren Kierkegaard and Thomas Merton both discussed the idea of a "true self," an authentic way of being who we were *intended* to be.[2] Merton clearly laid out the difficulty of the process of discovering who we are in God's eyes: "Real self-conquest is the conquest of ourselves not by ourselves but by the Holy Spirit. Self-conquest is really self-surrender. Yet before we can surrender ourselves, we must become ourselves. For no one can give up what he does not possess."[3]

At every turn Scripture tells stories of faithful folks who wrestled with self-doubts and insecurity. Immediately after telling the widow at Zarephath not to be afraid, Elijah trembled at Queen Jezebel's threat (1 Kings 19:3). Jonah struggled with insecurity and discouragement. He was so overcome by his unhealthy self-interest that he wished he would die even after God's demonstration of compassion and forgiveness to Israel's enemy, the Ninevites (Jon 4:1-8). Moses, Gideon, and King Saul were all keenly aware of their personal and social limitations (Ex 3:11; 4:10; Judg 6:15; 1 Sam 9:21).

The Bible calls Christlikeness being "conformed to the image of his Son" (Rom 8:29). I don't know too many people who naturally want to conform to much of anything. We don't like to change. Conforming requires a form or a mold, and that often means squeezing into something. In the process some parts are left out. Conforming restricts us; it chisels away our excesses and requires periods of setting in the new mold. Conforming opposes our will, with its wants and wishes, and yet it's in conforming that we are fashioned in Christ's likeness.

If we're honest, we have to acknowledge that we're always conforming to something. Culture is like a water park's lazy river, moving us along its self-focused consumeristic current. Our family of origin instilled in us values that we either conform to or intentionally work against. We're influenced by the people we spend time with and the books we read. We are always conforming to something or to someone, even when it feels like we're sitting still or stuck. It's just that we need to reflect on the direction we're conforming to.

Robert Mulholland said it better:

We are being shaped into either the wholeness of the image of Christ or a horrible destructive caricature of that image—destructive not only to ourselves but also to others, for we inflict our brokenness upon them. This wholeness or destructiveness radically conditions our relationship with God, ourselves and others, as well as our involvement in the dehumanizing structures of the broken world around us. We become either agents of God's healing and liberating grace or carriers of the sickness of the world.[4]

Conforming to Christ is not about doing more or gaining more; we can't lift ourselves up by our bootstraps, the American default to solving most problems. And better self-esteem isn't the answer either. We are to be conformed in our hearts to Jesus, to live out Christ's transformation so that his power is evident to a world bored to tears by religiosity and sectarianism, and looking for a deeper and hope-giving version of Christianity. That is found in Jesus and in our enduring (or "abiding") closeness to him (Jn 15).

Through the eyes of Jesus we begin to see ourselves as we truly are—beloved, deeply loved, cherished, forgiven, and gifted. The first blind spot is cleared when we draw close to Jesus, experience his loving forgiveness, and surrender to his leading. In his presence conforming is built on trust, not obligation.

The Bible describes an outcome of spending time with Jesus as an aroma. As we draw close to God in prayer, read his Word, begin to see the world as he does, choose and talk about subjects like he did, and care for others as he did, we begin to smell like him. Before you laugh, imagine that the disciples literally would have had the aroma of the places they walked with Jesus: the fields, the vineyard, the crowds. And Paul got more specific: "We are to God the pleasing aroma of Christ among those who are being saved and those who are perishing" (2 Cor 2:15). *We are the aroma of Christ.* Our lives (how we act and what we say) are to be a fragrant testimony to the person and essential qualities of Christ and of his good news to the world. In fact, some commentators say that Christ is the Savior that is exhaling in our lives and work.

This imagery places responsibility on us for integrity and charity of the deepest measure. It demands humility and an enthusiastic pledge to Christ, not just as the source of life but as the ongoing, life-giving presence in our lives. All of the strategies, skills, and self-awareness we can learn are secondary to the fundamental source of nurture in our lives, the abiding presence of Christ. Nothing is produced without the connection to the Vine, no lasting fruit, nothing (Jn 15:5). We can till the soil, but the fragrance has a divine source.

We've all tried to be the source too many times. We've learned to project a particular image to others (we use our personality to accomplish things), to craft and create a false yet productive self. And then we devote ourselves to sustain and defend this false self. David Benner explains, "The false self is like the air we breathe" and suggests that few things are more difficult to dismantle than the illusions we've lived with for so long.[5] He notes that most of us possess "an inordinate attachment to an image of ourselves that makes us special."[6] That external image gets things done and produces results, which is usually how we measure our ministry effectiveness—but this is very different from being so close to Jesus that our ministry is recognized by his aroma.

Too often we attend to externals such as skills, gifts, capacity, and entrepreneurial spirit, so much so that our spiritual life atrophies, inhibiting our maturation and personal development. Atrophied muscles take time, energy, and discipline to get into shape. Likewise, learning how to remain close to Jesus, be honest with ourselves and others, live in authentic community with others, and develop gracious ways in our relationships requires a high level of discipline and regular moments of fresh perspective.

OUR REACTIONS ARE THE KEY

As we gain experience in working with others, how do we (hopefully) become more aware of our particular gifts and motivations?

How can we experience such a Christ-centered transformation that we are freed from measuring ourselves against an illusion of others' success, a wisp that dances about and can never be caught? Fortunately there's a simple practice that I will mention throughout the entire book. It will require gut-level honesty on your part and openness to what God wants to do in your life.

I want you to <u>pay attention to how you</u> *react*, including those deep down internal reactions that no one else sees. When I coach leaders about their personal development, I tell them to take an imaginary reaction selfie whenever they react to something.[7] Anytime we have a reaction, even those unseen by others, imagine we catch it on camera and store it for later reflection. Reactions are raw; they're in-the-moment responses that flow unfiltered from deep within our being. Sometimes the selfie reveals the raise of an eyebrow, a tightening shoulder, or scratching an ear. Sometimes it's like leaking steam, other times a sweet fragrance, and still others it erupts like molten lava. If we want to listen, our reactions are telling us a story we need to hear.

SELF-CHECK

When you have time for reflection, look at that reaction selfie and ask yourself these questions:

- Why did I react that way?
- What desires does that reaction reveal?
- What are the sources or causes for those desires?
- Do those reflect the desires of Christ?
- What does God require of me in regards to the reasons for that reaction?

If you are willing to learn more, you can ask others around you what they notice about your reactions. We all watch each other, but we don't usually say anything about what we notice. If we give each other permission to share, we might learn a lot.

For instance, I am learning to be careful of my nonverbal reactions. My wife is a visual learner and can read nonverbals like a Jedi. Over the years she has worked with me to recognize that I need to pay attention to what my expressions and posture are communicating, which may be different from what I intend. I had a friend in college tell me that I looked mad whenever my mind was elsewhere. My face let people know that I was not fully present in the moment (more on this topic later in the book).

Years ago coal miners used to take a caged canary with them deep into the mine. If the canary, with its smaller lungs, died, the miners knew there wasn't much oxygen left and that they should immediately get out. In the same way, our reactions might be telling how much life we have left in various areas of our lives. Reactions are telling, and can reveal three elements residing deep within us.

Reactions expose our insecurities. For example, Jeremy gets anxious every time his boss comes into his office and closes the door. Often the reason is to share something confidential or to block out the noise in the hallway. But early in his career Jeremy had a boss who walked into his office only to scold him. It's a decade later, but Jeremy is still afraid of what might happen.

Reactions reveal our ego. Our reactions reveal much about our identity and desires. For example, I occasionally get an email from recent graduates who are new to their ministry setting. They vent to me about a situation they're involved in. The notes are full of raw frustrations, rich with honesty. Thirty minutes later I usually get an "I'm sorry" email. But I don't mind. I love these rare expressions of real honesty, which are opportunities to step out from behind the self-protective masks. I try to help these leaders discover what their reactions might be telling them.

Reactions affirm our hopes. If reactions come from our heart, then they show us where we have set our affections. Reactions show us when we're being blocked (like a slow driver in front of us), what we want, and where we place our trust. When we're faced with moments of suffering and our first reaction is to seek God's face, we are seeing evidence of spiritual growth.

UNSPOKEN PEOPLE PROBLEMS

I want to highlight some common reactions that we don't often see discussed in leadership circles, but nonetheless are notorious people problems. They may be private and no one else notices, or they may be blatantly apparent to others but we don't notice them. It's common to see leaders with people problems, but those around them don't know how to bring up these problems. In fact, it's likely they aren't even sure we're interested in hearing about them. That's why your own interest and effort are crucial as you read this book. These areas require an *intentional* glance into our blind spot. I know some of our problems have the illusion of being nonissues, but like a rip tide beneath the ocean's surface, their presence is warning us that we need to address their source before something gives way and we're pulled in too deep.

"I am the boss." This one is tricky because, for many of us, we *are* the boss; we are expected to lead and make decisions. But what does "being the boss" mean? When we have that reaction, what's going on? Leaders are to be in charge, yet we need to avoid the practice of insulating ourselves from criticism. And this is where the reaction is serving like the canary, telling us about our insecurity, pride, or dreams.

Over time, leading tempts us to spend energy protecting our leadership rather than serving the people we lead. But we don't need any more examples of what happens to leaders when they feel they're above others. I challenge you to find examples of Christian leaders who insulated themselves from others, felt they were above others, been unable to share responsibility or vulnerability with others, and ended up exemplary in substance and conduct throughout and in the end. Often the only thing supporting those with puffed-up importance is hot air.

Ironically, as I wrote this section I had an email that prompted this very reaction in me. Someone wanted to see the components of one of my ministry areas to suggest potential changes. My initial reaction was one of "that's *my* area. I'm in charge there." I was less concerned about a better direction and outcome for my people and program, and instead was more focused on self-protection. *Wow.* So if I took a reaction selfie, it would help me recognize the tight grip I hold on both my pride and insecurities. The "I'm the boss" reaction is less about the future and greater fruitfulness and more about control and protecting reputation. Scripture reminds us of the Christlike way here: "In humility value others above yourselves, not looking to your own interests but each of you to the interests of the others" (Phil 2:3-4).

"I'm the smartest person in the room." Leadership smarts may not equal leadership maturity, and knowing facts does not equal intelligence. There's an old adage that high IQ gets you promoted, but low emotional intelligence (EQ) gets you fired. Long-term leadership effectiveness is less about knowledge or experience and more about the graces we share with those around us. This reaction might be a canary telling you that you've stopped growing in your leadership and are too reliant on what your abilities can accomplish. Grace is to be a characteristic of us as Christian leaders, and we should "not think of yourself more highly than you ought, but rather think of yourself with sober judgment" (Rom 12:3).

SELF-CHECK

Take a quick checklist assessment to see if any of these are true:

- Do you have positive thoughts about the people you're leading?
- Is there growing participation from those you lead?
- Would you say there is a growing interest in where your group is going?
- Can you identify a potential replacement for your position?
- Are people affirming you on a regular basis?
- Are you affirming others on a regular basis?

If you answered no to any of these, it would be worth your attention and that of your leadership team or a group of spiritually mature friends.

"You can't say that to me." Do you have that person around you who is always defensive? I had such a friend, and one day I watched him make presentations in three different meetings. During each of those meetings, people offered ideas that would have helped his project immensely and made it easy to implement. No matter, he strongly defended himself against each simply because someone was opposing him. I eventually became his supervisor and learned that if I weathered his initial response, the next day he'd warm to my suggestion after a period of reflection.

I know this reaction all too well because I'm defensive at times. I've discovered that my defensiveness is strongest when my ego and identity feel threatened or my way forward is being blocked. Most of us do this. The lesson I need to learn is that God is at work in my life and he is my defender, something that the psalmist reminds himself of over and over. God wants me to see my whole life as his work—

and his to protect. The fiery Paul writes a very nondefensive prescription for life in Romans 12:14-19:

> Bless those who persecute you; bless and do not curse. Rejoice with those who rejoice; mourn with those who mourn. Live in harmony with one another. Do not be proud, but be willing to associate with people of low position. Do not be conceited.
>
> Do not repay anyone evil for evil. Be careful to do what is right in the eyes of everyone. If it is possible, as far as it depends on you, live at peace with everyone. Do not take revenge, my dear friends, but leave room for God's wrath, for it is written: "It is mine to avenge; I will repay," says the Lord.

"I'm better than they are." This reaction is most common when we enter a group, room, or conference and perform a quick assessment. We rank ourselves based on unsophisticated and uninformed criteria. These might include appearance, age, personality type, job titles, or reputation. It's what leadership coach and Irving Bible Church pastor David Grant calls the "better than" syndrome: we feel good about ourselves simply because we think we're better than those around us.[8] National ministry leader Jason Jensen added, "And our tendency to do this, in my experience, is greater in at least two situations: When the group is impressive or competitive, and when we actually feel insecure about being judged by them, especially because we actually respect them."[9]

Paul recognized this tendency too, and told the Galatians, "Make a careful exploration of who you are and the work you have been given, and then sink yourself into that. Don't be impressed with yourself. Don't compare yourself with others. Each of you must take responsibility for doing the creative best you can with your own life" (Gal 6:4-5 *The Message*).

Too often I see young adults stop growing and moving forward once they determine they're "better than." What if that standard is too low? What if God wants to call us to something that demands daily courage beyond what we've needed to date? Too often a "better than" syndrome causes us to settle for something less than our best— it's just that we believe we're better than others around us.

"I will just avoid them." Unfortunately, resentment is too common in Christian ministries and churches. We have people who aren't talking to each other and aren't interested in bridging the divide. Too many in Christian work step over the hurting along the road hoping someone else will be the good Samaritan. If we came to visit your group or church, would we find more instances of people avoiding others than anyone would care to admit or know? These passive-aggressive undercurrents will be dealt with in chapter seven, but if you react by avoiding others, there is often a spirit of entitlement, competition, and pride. If we look to Jesus Christ as our model, we see a very different mission. Jesus never avoided people. In fact, he sought out people to serve and love.

"It's not my fault." We sat in a circle at a conference, a group of eight leaders of various ages from all over the country. The youngest in the group spoke first (this happens often, doesn't it?) and asked two quick questions of the group, not waiting long for answers. As the rest of us were forming the answers in our minds, he blurted, "I feel frustrated. I'm the hardest working staff member in the ministry, and I feel like we're stuck. And I'm not getting the support I need." The collective inhale of the group was noticeable, and there was an awkward pause. One of the older pastors in the group seized the moment and, with great wisdom and skill, shared with the young leader how his comment sounded.

In our culture it's natural to blame others for our problems. We blame parents for all sorts of things, teachers (or students) for what's going on with education, the government for various social conditions, busyness for our lack of performance, and bosses for problems at work. The blame game is one of the hardest to spot because our therapeutic culture has championed the search for external reasons for our problems. Certainly, many of us have been wounded deeply, are enduring external problems that limit us, and carry many types of scars that need healing—some from our family of origin.

College students Victor and Andrew sat next to each other in a class about leadership. Victor was an All-American college athlete, participated in a comedy group at the school, and spent Sundays as a part-time youth director in a local church. Andrew was largely uninvolved at the school, yet he had difficulties turning assignments in on time or even showing up to class. While the busier Victor was meeting all of the requirements, Andrew would say to me, "Sorry I didn't get that paper in on time, but it's been a busy week." Or "I couldn't make it to class today. Yeah, uh, I wasn't feeling well." I had noticed this pattern for a while and recognized it as one I had to work on while in college, so I set up a private conversation with Andrew. His first response was, "Sorry, yeah, it's been a tough year." He went on to explain about his parents' problems and his own financial burdens and added, "If you gave me more time, I would be able to get the work done."

So, I did.

But he didn't.

Andrew couldn't hear his continuous excuses, putting the fault on someone or something else. His excuses felt very real to him, but in reality some had commonsense solutions. It took months before he was able to dig deeper with me to discover the pattern and see that there was an issue that required professional counseling. He eventually took that step and was able to make the necessary changes, though too late for some of those classes. If he would have been more honest and self-aware earlier, his trajectory might be very different than it was.

The presence of *but* or *if* in our conversations signal that we need to pay better attention. Are we excusing ourselves for things we shouldn't? Have you ever said or thought, "I would give my teaching more effort if the people would just pay more attention" or "I would pray more if it made a difference"? Those are two that I've heard recently, and certainly I use some that I'm not aware of. We need to pay attention to how we think we'd be more successful if someone else would get their act together. We need to note how often we excuse a lack of effort or excellence due to busyness or personal problems. And then we can prayerfully discern the real cause behind our excuse.

SELF-CHECK

When we blame, we usually aren't truthful, and instead we divert attention to other sources for our level of commitment or work. For instance, do a quick integrity inventory:

- Is your yes a yes, or do you change the truth, even just a bit, to make yourself look good?
- Is your blame accurate, or might God want you to take steps toward solving the situation?
- Does your blame regularly hide things from others? From family or friends?
- If you blame busyness, spend ten minutes with paper and pen and make a column of anything that you have been putting off. In a second column list other things you've accomplished while you've been procrastinating. Think about why the second column's work got done while the first column's work remained undone.
- If you visited a counselor and they heard your blame, would they think it came from jealousy, envy, or pride?

THERE'S NO COMPARISON

Seeing ourselves for who we are created to be means that we need to take our eyes off of others for our definition of success or failure. Paying attention to our reactions is a powerful way to clear the blind spots and honestly see our self. In my early days of ministry I thought I was doing well because I was inching up the leadership ladder recognized within Christian ministry circles. At the same time the relationships with those I worked with every day were heading the other direction. The ladder I was climbing was leaning against the wrong wall.[10] Only when that ladder was knocked out from under my feet did I become aware of the issues, comparisons, and blaming that I had unknowingly engaged in.

Do you struggle with the grace-killing temptation of comparison? Do you blame other things or people for situations? Don't attempt to be anything other than what God desires. Be the real you. There's no comparison!

Let Bob Laurent's words to me encourage us all: "Don't try to be like someone else. What we need is you. What your people need is what God has done in you and your passion. You give your best and don't try to be anyone else."

FOR GREATER AWARENESS

1. What makes you feel defensive? When were the last two times you felt a high level of insecurity? What events triggered those feelings? Is there a pattern to these moments? If so, what do you think it reveals about your defensiveness?

2. Who did you compete with for attention with in school, work, or home? Who or what do you find yourself competing with these days? Is the answer the same? Have you ever talked with the person (or people) about the competition? Why or why not?

3. Are you satisfied or dissatisfied with your gifts and abilities? What qualities or abilities do you see in others that you wish you could possess? Has anyone talked to you about gifts and abilities you have that they desire? Do you respond by acknowledging the compliment or by arguing?

4. Spend a week and pay particular attention to your reactions. Imagine taking a selfie of your reactions. As you identify them, within a few hours spend fifteen minutes journaling about it. Then talk with a trusted friend within the next day about what you wrote, asking your friend to help you learn something about yourself through this example.

5. Read Matthew 23. Then get a good commentary and read the section on that chapter. Note any verses that connect well to the themes of this chapter, and then rewrite them in your own words as if you were paraphrasing the meaning so that others would understand it better.

6. Write down the names of people you admire. Next to each one, list the characteristics or attributes you find admirable. If you haven't already, consider handwriting them a note (not email or text message) of thanks for being a faithful model for you. Be sure to let them know what you admire.

3

MY MOTHER DIED SUDDENLY when I was almost ten years old. My life turned upside down. One day she came home from the doctor with a diagnosis of leukemia. Seven days later she disappeared to her bedroom and extended family was called in. I only saw her once more during the next three days because the disease's emaciating effects were clear. That visit was my last image of her as I awoke two days later on Sunday morning to the sounds of her taking her last gasp of breath.

It seemed to happen as quickly as this paragraph could be read. One minute she was here, the next she was gone. The shock and grief made home tense at times, which is only normal. Food lost its taste. Routines weren't routine anymore. My sister, dad, and I had to find a way forward as a family. My dad, a pastor, was a strong help during those days of loss and pain, even as he faced his own grief. Those who have grieved deeply know that the emptiness comes and goes like waves; some days were better than others. Even years later. Grieving never truly ends, it just takes on different hues.

Mom's passing left me with a choice: move toward a deeper Christian faith amid the grief or shake my fist at God for what I was going through. My early adolescent years nurtured fresh abandonment to Jesus and awareness that each day was to be savored and lived to its fullest—not for personal achievement or the applause of others, but for its God-honoring quality and opportunity. I understood that each season of life sets lessons before us that we are to learn and that life is a blip on the timeline of eternity.

Another outcome of Mom's passing was a persistent loneliness that was my companion throughout my adolescence and into my adult years. It wasn't constant, but it could suddenly overwhelm me for a day. Some days I pursued it, my artsy personality relishing its gray and melancholy ways. Or if I am honest, the lonely feelings provided a way to still feel my loss. I could be in a crowd of people or on a sunny family bike ride and still feel a lonely isolation that weighed me down. Everyone around seemed holographic and distant, like moving shadows on walls, and I had disappeared into a world of confusion, like Frodo putting on the ring.

This chapter deals with our past, a persistent blind spot for Christian leaders. We all have gone through success, failure, pain, and joy that have reinforced or pushed us in particular directions. The social and mental scripts and frameworks we use for dealing with those moments have given emotional and behavioral shape to our social lives. Where did we learn how to respond to adversity or celebrate with others? How did we learn how to show affection, handle success, make friends, be a part of a group, or participate in social functions? What role have our experiences played in developing our personalities?

Some of you have experienced deep pain, abuse, and other hurtful situations. You already know the pain; it is not a blind spot.

There are many good resources and counselors who can help, and I prayerfully encourage you to turn to them before moving ahead here. To be clear, this chapter does not minimize those hurtful realities but rather focuses on the social side of our past and the way it affects our present ministry.

LIKE GOING BACK TO HIGH SCHOOL

Meg Greenfield was a longtime Washington, DC, columnist and editor. In the final two years of her life she wrote a memoir, which wasn't published until after her death, about her work and the government. In the book, *Washington*, she shared how surprised she was at the similarities between the social dynamics of the US government and those found in a local high school.[1] That doesn't give us much political confidence perhaps, and may answer more than a few questions we've had about government, but it illustrates how powerful the patterns learned in high school can be, even for those asked to lead a powerful country. Yet we don't talk about it much. Who really wants someone to tell them they make choices and interact with others like a high schooler? Yet how many times have you heard someone, even those well-advanced in age, share that they're still trying to figure out what they want to do in life "when I grow up"? And how often do conversations in board meetings begin to reflect high school lunchrooms?

Problems and patterns from the past show up in various ways, and not just in Washington. Harry was an itinerant speaker, traveling along as a guest speaker with large groups on summer mission trips. One week he went on a trip with four church groups. Each day the groups would go out on several projects, and Harry would get to spend time with the students on the trip. At night he'd speak as part of a program and be available for any pastoral counseling. It was all going very well until one of the older pastors pulled him aside.

"Harry," the pastor from Alabama said, "I want to talk with you privately about something." This already sounded ominous. "I've noticed that you're spending most of your time with a few of my more popular students." Harry flinched as the pastor continued, "In fact, as I've watched you, wherever Megan, Deb, and Jake go, you're not too far away. Now, there's nothing wrong with that, but it did catch my attention, and I wanted to privately let you know."

At first Harry was stunned and a bit angry that this stranger was bringing this stuff up. Megan was stunning and easily the most popular young woman on the trip because of it. Deb and Jake were just so fun to be around. Harry felt alive when he was with them and Megan, like he was young again. Harry began to realize that he had an opportunity to share with this wise and caring pastor. He smiled ruefully and asked, "Can I talk with you? I mean, *really* talk?"

Harry shared that he had been noticing how his past was affecting his current ministry, that God had been showing him this recently. Speaking to teens gave Harry a platform; he enjoyed the laughs and loved the affirmation of seeing God work in their lives. Hanging around students when not on the stage was the problem, however. Just as happened in high school, his insecurities kick in as he wondered what the teens were thinking of him up close. He wanted to feel accepted, and the fact that pretty and popular students like Megan paid attention to him fueled his sense of self-worth and made him feel good as a young man. And sometimes, if he was honest, he felt himself attracted to Megan (and others like her on other trips). He was careful about how he acted around the teens, but he knew his thoughts, and he knew how they made him feel.

It was clear that Harry had to address this area. Grateful that someone had taken a step to carefully confront him, he promised to spend time with all of the teens on the trip. He and the pastor crafted a plan for Harry to prayerfully explore with his wife and a counselor what was going on in this area. A year later Harry gave up his speaking ministry and took a lead pastor position at a church. And he is thriving in that role to this day.

Before we judge Harry, let's admit that we all have past memories and experiences that shape our current preferences and practices. It may be more than insecurity that we're attracted to people we are supposed to be ministering to; the research on extended adolescence suggests that we arrive at ministry in our twenties with some unfinished business regarding our identity, sense of purpose, and maybe other deeper issues. Developmental expert Laurence Steinberg (and others) say that young adults in the workforce (including vocational ministry) are still developing and preparing for adulthood.[2] Our past holds significant blind spots that influence why we make some of our choices, work toward particular goals, and make preferences among our relationships. And most leaders do not seek pastors or mentors to help them work through those areas. The problems are carried well into adulthood.

> Our past holds significant blind spots that influence why we make some of our choices, work toward particular goals, and make preferences among our relationships.

An easy way to recognize how the past intersects with our present is to pay attention to why we avoid certain people or places. Some of us talk too much about our past, reminding everyone of historical successes. Others want to avoid thinking about it altogether. And most of us are unaware of the effect that our growing-up days had on us, and perhaps still do. We are shaped by our past but not fully aware of how powerful it can be. In the rest of this chapter we will get a biblically based glimpse of struggles with the past and then address reasons for our responses so we're not stuck relating and leading like we did in high school.

GOD IS INTERESTED IN REDEEMING YOUR PAST

One of my favorite scenes in Scripture shows Moses standing in front of a bush on fire but not being consumed, and God is speaking from the center of the bush. Moses was leaning on a well-worn, wooden staff. God asks Moses to lay it down, to let it drop to the dust before him, to surrender the staff, which had been his support for his work as he navigated the countryside (Ex 3–4). It's his protection, his instrument of work, his identity as one who tended to animals.

Moses was at the bush because he had run away. He had stepped out of an Egyptian palace one day to walk among his people, the Hebrews. He caught sight of a Hebrew being beaten by an Egyptian. Moses may have seen the moment he could be used of God to rescue the Israelites. He attacked and killed the Egyptian, but the Israelites did not share his redemptive perspective on his leadership role. Moses fled into the wilderness, started a family, and took up life in obscurity working for his father-in-law, Jethro (Acts 7:23-29). It was a long period of following sheep before Moses came to the burning bush. God was about to set Moses on a new mission to confront Pharaoh and lead the Israelites out of Egypt. But now, in front of the great I AM, his past, with its memories, disappointment, fears, and guilt, came flooding back.

Woven throughout Scripture are regular reminders that we are to let go of the past. We are reminded that God wants to forgive, restore, and redeem our lives for his purposes. Like Moses, we come to moments where our past floods into our present. We don't know Moses' thoughts there in the wilderness, but it's likely he revisited the murder scene and remembered again the failed dream of rescuing the Israelites from Egypt's rule. His concern about his poor communication skills may reflect that moment when his inability to explain his mission meant he left Egypt for decades. The man who was once full of confidence stood crushed and insecure under his memories. He stood in front of the I AM who was ready to use Moses to realize that dream again but under new management.

Let's leave Moses there in front of God as we look at another biblical model. I mentioned Paul's statement about forgetting the past and pressing on (Phil 3:13). But this statement doesn't mean that Paul never thought about the past, nor does it mean that he wasn't shaped by his past. At the church in Galatia he used his past stories to give context for his current, grace-oriented ministry. He describes the value of seeing our past from God's perspective (Col 3:1-4), because God has a history of wanting to do new things (Is 43:18-19) that are ways out of the barren places in our past and present lives. In several sermons and speeches, Paul describes his history before and after his conversation with Christ. And to fill in some of the gaps in Paul's past, God guides Luke to describe them in the book of Acts.

The best way to describe God's approach to our past is that God wants us to remember the work that he has done in our past (search for the word *remember* in the Bible and notice its purpose), but we cannot let our past impede the present work of God (2 Cor 5:17). And we need to take seriously the "new creation" work that God has done in our lives and accept that the old has passed away.

Despite our desire to be comfortable, we develop spiritual maturity and perseverance through the trials, pain, and even temptations of life. Through the pains of our past, God seeks to develop spiritual maturity in the present, resulting in our knowing him intimately, becoming like him, and serving him (Rom 5:1-5; Jas

1:2-5). For those who've been hanging on to guilt for many years, this is perhaps the most difficult. We all regret past behavior and thoughts that we wish we could go back and correct, but we can't. We also can't carry these into the future. *Today is the day to let go and realize that God offers his forgiveness and restoration.* There is no longer any condemnation or accusation (Ps 103:8-12; Rom 8:1).

This is the wonder that Jesus brought to those weighed down by the religiosity of the Pharisees. Jesus offered redemption and forgiveness, not a constant reminder of how people didn't measure up. He was the new standard, not the law. He first offered love. When people like the woman caught in adultery and Zacchaeus encountered Jesus, their experience wasn't accusation but redemption. With Jesus, they named the wrongs in their past, confessed, and found the freedom to move on. The Zacchaeus, a tax collector, gleefully paid back all that he had taken and more, in an obedient act of contrition (Lk 19:8-9). The woman stood from the dust, no stones coming down on her head (Jn 8:10-11). In advance, each understood the message Jesus would leave with his disciples on that last evening before his death, "If you love me, you will obey what I command" (Jn 14:15).

Let's go back to Moses, standing in front of God. The burning-bush story is very familiar, but I love the way it's depicted in the animated movie *The Prince of Egypt*. In that movie the voice asks Moses to pick up the staff. When Moses does, the voice then says, "With this staff, you will do my wonders!" That's what we do in ministry. We lay down our lives with our history, memory, and pain, and we let God's forgiveness and grace do their cleansing work. Then God commands us to go, and with our lives and gifts, we will do his wonders. And wonders we will see as people put their trust in Christ, as they grow in that trust, and as they in turn minister in the lives of others.

A CLEAR VIEW OF THE PAST

In my coaching of younger leaders, I've discovered four blind spots from the past common to those in ministry leadership. You may be tempted to skim over them lightly. Don't. Linger a bit on each, asking God for clarity, and allowing time to reflect and consider each. While you do, remember that God wants to redeem your past and even use it for his work and glory.

Drive for popularity. Harry's story is just one of many that show us the desire to be popular is not often quenched once we leave school. If we aren't careful, it can consume us, even into our retirement years. We *want* to fit in. We *want* to be accepted. And we *want* to be noticed.

I remember talking with my three kids about the opinions of others. No matter how eloquent I was, they chose what to wear, how to style their hair, and how to spend their free time in relation to what others at school were doing. Despite the stereotype that teens want to express individuality, on the high school campus we see the athletes, popular girls, and other subgroups all dress in similar fashion. At a time when individual expression is cherished, conformity won the struggle. Only after graduation do (many) students recognize how susceptible they were to the influence of their peers.

Is it that different for us as adults? Certainly, we rely on other's opinions to make us feel good about what we do and who we are. Social media, which most of us use, is built on the desire to be well-liked or well-followed. Are we satisfied with serving God where he has us, or do we seek a bigger audience in some way? If you attend any major Christian conference, you can probably identify those who are trying to be popular. They aren't just there to develop professionally; they are there to be known and affirmed by peers and by those in influential positions in particular. Henri Nouwen says the desire to be popular is a temptation common to

Christian leaders. He says we are tempted to make a difference for Jesus *and* are tempted to be popular, spectacular, and relevant.[3] But Jesus wants his followers to be different. Our desire to be great, or popular, is to be replaced by a spirit of servanthood and sacrifice (Lk 22:25-26). He challenged those who were drawn to his popularity: "Whoever wants to be my disciple must deny themselves and take up their cross daily and follow me. For whoever wants to save their life will lose it, but whoever loses their life for me will save it. What good is it for someone to gain the whole world, and yet lose or forfeit their very self?" (Lk 9:23-25).

There is a subtler response to popularity, one that is less easily recognized but has the same proud rooting. We can condemn and avoid the popular people, withdrawing (well, protecting ourselves, really) from "putting ourselves out there." Some of us learned in our teenage years to shun the popular crowd, either because of thinking that we were in some way superior to them or feeling awkward to be with them. And we still do it in adulthood. We protect ourselves from social harm and discomfort. And, in an unfortunate blend of pride and insecurity, little communities of criticism are formed that take aim at the popular and successful. So we must guard against either seeking popularity ourselves or looking negatively at those who travel in those circles.

The burden of past relationships. From our past to right now, we've developed strong patterns and preferences for social interaction. The people you were drawn to in your youth are likely the kinds of people you will be comfortable with it in adulthood. The people who intimidated you in high school likely do the same in adulthood. The types of people you didn't like in high school may also pose difficulties for you as an adult.

This may seem implausible to you, but I've seen pastors hesitant to work with confident, driven business people in their

SELF-CHECK

Here are three practices to help you reduce the desire for popularity:

First, develop a deep thirst for understanding your identity in Christ by studying Scripture. Through God's Word we see ourselves as he does and understand that he transforms our lives—and that's the greatest confidence builder we can have. The letter to the Colossians provides a powerful story of who Christ is, who he makes us to be, and how we are to live.

Second, listen for thoughts about yourself that begin with "I always" or "I am just," and listen to how you finish them. To challenge yourself, start a page in your journal and write fifty answers to those phrases. As you look at the list, how many of the items are comparative, are rooted in gaps between the popular (or unpopular) people and you, and how many are unfounded self-judgments?

Finally, reflect on your interaction with crowds. Make a list of your interactions in groups for the past week. Ask yourself, and God, how often you felt good because popular groups paid attention to you? How often did you feel hurt because someone ignored a comment you made? How often did you see interactions as ways to make you feel better rather than ways to make someone else feel better?

churches because of adolescent-like insecurity. I've seen people in ministry avoid different community groups because the social dynamics scared them. I've watched people in ministry avoid youth who were the kind they avoided during high school. Some of us know that we avoid certain settings because we don't want to see a person from our past. And some avoid events because we don't want to meet people we've had conflicts with (see chapter seven).

Emirose, a friend of mine, avoided a campus where she had previously worked because she didn't want to run into Jean. Jean had been responsible for a process that cost Emirose and several of her coworkers their jobs. After eight or nine years, well-established in a new career, Emirose discovered she had to get a key from Jean for an event on campus. Emirose realized that it was time to let God heal the pain of the past. The two women talked briefly, Emirose acknowledging how much she had been annoyed with Jean. The two never became friends, but they acknowledged the healing that God had done. And Emirose was comfortable on the campus thereafter.

You and I are called to minister to others with a newfound freedom from the past.

SELF-CHECK

The following are three practices that can help us find that freedom.

First, go back to the list of interactions from the last week. Who do you seek out, avoid, or wish to spend time with? After thinking about past relationships, do you see any patterns? Where do those patterns come from? How might the Holy Spirit want to work in your life in a new way?

Second, make a list of two or three names of people you are avoiding. (You can ask God to help you with this.) In a couple sentences, write why you are avoiding them, and then suggest what kind of freedom you would find by making peace in these relationships.

Third, if you recognize an issue (perhaps you react to something and you *know* it comes from an incident in your past), talk with a trusted, godly friend, life coach, or a counselor about how to resolve it.

Fourth, celebrate the relationships you do have. Ask God for a couple ways to deepen your present relationships to keep them healthy.

Past performances. Occasionally I like to watch *Napoleon Dynamite*, an old and odd movie depicting very rural high school life in the Western Plains states of America. A few scenes show Uncle Rico videotaping himself throwing a football while recounting his football days. He always bragged that if he could go back in time he would win the state championship. Visit any major sporting event at your local high school and you'll see adults like Uncle Rico reliving their glory days.

Ministry is not an extension of your high school experiences. It is not an opportunity to live out your youth again through the lives of another. It is not a platform for you to share your story with others or merely an opportunity to steer others from the mistakes you've made by talking at length about your failures. It is focused on others and their stories in the present, helping them love God with all of their heart, soul, mind, and might. It is about seeing them grow to greater Christian maturity and faithfulness to what Jesus would have them think, say, and do.

> Ministry is not an extension of your high school experiences or merely an opportunity to steer others from the mistakes you've made.

If you are living your present ministry based on or bound by your successes and failures in the past, you are being shaped by a blind spot. But this isn't just about the past of five years ago. You are right now creating a reputation that will be your past five years from now. If we are living in the past, our present will be of little benefit to the future.

I want to give you three cautionary examples of ways that you are currently shaping your future past. First, social media has made hiring potential leaders a bit easier for interview committees. By the time someone shows up for an interview, committee members may have read through years of status updates, photos, and comments to guess what kind of person the candidate was and maybe is. I feel like I'm stating the obvious here, but you need to be very careful what you do and say online. It reflects who you are, who you want to be, and what you value.

Second, be aware of the volatile nature of pranks. An adolescent practice, pranks have little or no place in Christian ministry leadership. Pranks aren't practiced by community leaders—and those of us in Christian ministry are community leaders. In the last year I have heard three stories from ministry leaders I know well who thought pranking or extreme horseplay would be fun. The police were called in all three instances, and injuries required hospitalization in two of them. Once the stories were leaked to the community, the responses were a collective, "What were they thinking?"

Boards, committees, and supervisors have problems knowing how to work with maturity problems that surface in young leaders. Please understand that ministries committed to developing Christlike maturity in their people can't tolerate poor decision patterns in their leaders.

> Boards, committees, and supervisors have problems knowing how to work with maturity problems that surface in young leaders. Please understand that ministries committed to developing Christlike maturity in their people can't tolerate poor decision patterns in their leaders.

Finally, how a person handles discomfort is telling. In our culture we are emotionally wired for happiness and work hard to protect and sustain our good feelings. In the face of discomfort we whine, complain, and work to avoid the problem (or others). Mature leaders can function despite discomfort, and they stick to a job until it is finished. They can put up with unpleasantness and frustration; they give more than is asked, help without prompting, and make independent decisions.

I have an axiom: *having good people solves many problems*. I remember commenting about a young Christian worker I had hired: "I just like the choices he makes." Only two years into vocational ministry he was showing good intuition. We demonstrate our intuition by the choices we make. If the past is adversely influencing how we act in public, then we need to see the patterns before it's too late.

SELF-CHECK

The following are three practices to help you think about the past performance blind spot:

First, what stories of your past have you told in the past week? Are you still trying to be the person you were then, or are the stories becoming stories of what God is doing?

Second, look back through your Facebook or Instagram feeds for the last week. If someone had to write a description of your values based only on those words, pictures, and shares, what story would they tell? Are you happy with that story? How could you change it?

Third, how is God calling you to use your life choices to guide the lives of people you are leading? What are two good changes you have seen in your life that are an example for others?

Past wounds. I've kept this practice for last because it can be the most tender. And I want to ease into it. I talked earlier about my running career. Runners cultivate a stride, based on the unique structure of their bones, ligaments, and muscles, all of which are shaped by their genetics. Our strides are all different; they are perfectly adapted to us.

But sometimes we are injured, so we change our stride and keep running. If we keep running without figuring out the nature of the injury and seeking healing, we can do permanent damage to ourselves, because our stride places stress on parts of our legs or hips or back not made to support running. Stopping to diagnose the reason for the limp is critical. A runner with a blister has a different problem from a runner with a fracture.

It's likely that you may be carrying some pain in your life. Some of these may be wounds from your past—regrets, loss, abuse, mistakes, misjudgments, bad relationships, and so on. The wounds of our lives often exist where our past intersects with our hearts, and we struggle deeply with emotional and spiritual health. We can cling to the pain and to excuses, or we can bury them deep, hoping they'll never be discovered. But they will. Actually, they already have been. God knows them and wants you to live victoriously. Left undiagnosed, these wounds change and cut our ministry stride to protect us from the pain.

Some of the people I work with have shared with me what others might call a "wounded heart." Emotional and spiritual growth is a struggle. Often, though our wound is long in the past, we still believe a set of lies that bind us. We hurt, or have been hurt, so we try to numb the pain through a variety of addictions. We escape from painful reality through excessive behavior. Pornography, drugs, Internet gaming, social media, OCD behaviors, illicit sex, and even achievement (busyness) are ways we try to forget, cope, or overcome.

The real problem is a wounded heart. No matter how much we work to modify, suppress, drown, or medicate wounds, we need a renovation of heart. We need to cry out to Jesus, confess where we've tried to be our own savior, and allow him to rule in all corners of our hearts.

To finish this section I'd like to suggest a heart review that goes back to the running image at the beginning of this section. Start with asking God to help you look clearly at your heart. Consider sitting with a trusted friend, conversation partner, or a mentor. And then use these questions as a review:

- Are the wounds you find like blisters? Do you need to look for small things that have created tender places?

- Are the wounds like pulled muscles, requiring some rest time and then the soul equivalent of a physical therapist?

- Are the wounds like fractures that need to be examined and set by a professional?

- Are the wounds catastrophic, needing immediate intervention?

One final thought about wounds. Sometimes our wounds have been healed, leaving only scars. The scar can remind of the old injury, or it can remind us of the touch of the Healer.

BREAK FREE

God often wants to speak to us in retrospect. Parker Palmer shares a discerning practice of asking, "What is your life trying to say to you?"[4] Once when I was in London I met my longtime friend Cristian from Eastern Europe, and we chatted about his work there. I could tell he was evaluating his job, and he gave off an air of resignation that he was stuck. Though in his early forties, he said, "You don't understand what it's like here. People get in their lane and then they just stay." His eyes drooped as he tried to smile a bit to assure me he was okay.

The problem with looking into our past is that we need wisdom—and sometimes God wants to take us out of our lane and move us into new possibilities. Too often we talk about possibilities and make them up ourselves. I'm talking about burning-bush moments when God wants to take what he's been doing in our lives to this point and propel us forward to something beyond what we can take claim for on our own.

What if our past is affecting our present and future more than we care to admit? I've been at this work of developing leaders too long to let this chapter close without one more moment to consider this. I've met enough leaders who are still operating in ways they can trace back to insecurity, hurt, unmet needs, lies they believe, or incidents they endured. It's time to break free, it's time to see yourself as God sees you, and it's time to step up to a new maturity in the present for the sake of your community. We've been called to shepherd others and lead. Let's be committed to Christ and to our best work in response to his calling. Let's lead forward with courage and conviction.

FOR GREATER AWARENESS

1. What is one experience from your past that now influences a behavior in the present? Is this a good behavior or one that needs to change? (You may want to pick something small rather than something traumatic.)

2. What's one thing from your past that you need to let go of and open your grip, giving it all to God? Like Moses, can you lay down your staff if God asks you to? What would that look like in your life?

3. Take some time for this exercise. In what ways has your heart been wounded? How has it healed? How has it not healed fully? How did you deal with that? How will you let God heal it?

4. As you think about how you thought and behaved in middle school, and your present interactions with others, do you think you are socially mature? What has helped you be this way? Can you teach and show others this way of life? How would you go about that?

5. What behaviors and attitudes are you making excuses for right now? Your excuses could be to God, to others, or even to yourself. What are the excuses you are making? What will it take to make the change that needs to be made?

4

WE DROVE UP TO THE ENTRANCE GATE, excited for the next few days in South Africa's Kruger National Park. Our goal was to see the "Big Five": lion, leopard, cape buffalo, elephant, and rhinoceros. I stepped out of the car to stretch my legs and take care of registration before driving to our campsite in Skukuza. Slowly, a guard walked up to me said with a northern Shona accent, "Sir, you must get back into the car. The lion, he will eat you." *Terry*, I thought, *you're not in America any more.*

All Kruger visitors are told to not to get out of the car when driving outside of the protected camps. Not long before our visit a park ranger had walked toward the end of one bridge thought to be in a safe zone. A leopard pounced out of the brush, dragged him back, and killed him. That story and a few YouTube videos were enough to keep us from any taking risks.

During my years of ministry and teaching I've noticed a "big five" set of temptations that stalk those in Christian ministry. They lurk along the paths of leadership, ready to run us over like a rhino or pull us to the side like the leopard. The temptations prey on our admirable qualities, using half-truths to lure us or pounce on our fears, pain, and insecurities, inviting us to explore more about who we are, and lying that we need to prove or numb ourselves in some way.

Almost everyone I know starts in ministry with the goal of serving God and helping others. We want to make an impact, to take charge, to be a provider, to have close and intimate relationships, and to be respected. These desires are admirable; if they weren't present in someone's life we probably wouldn't hire them for a ministry position. Over time, however, we can become complacent, inattentive, and, like the park ranger on the bridge, wander too far toward the path's edge, thinking we'll be okay. But we won't. Too many in Christian ministry have been devoured by temptations associated with these "big five": seeking prominence, holding on to control, valuing shiny stuff, pursuing inappropriate intimacy, and relishing resentment. Those big-five temptations surround our hopes, dreams, and wants, and draw us away by focusing our attention on what we lack. They are always lurking around the edges of our leadership lives.

One of the more helpful tools you can use while reading this book is the Enneagram. It has been around for years but has had a recent surge in popularity due to the wonderful book *The Road Back to You*.[1] The Enneagram will reveal your dominant personality type, your reactions under stress, and even your primary temptations. I recommend taking the more comprehensive test (it's not that expensive) at enneagraminstitute.com. Doing so was a very revealing and helpful process for me and for many of my friends.

SEEKING PROMINENCE

I remember encountering one of the big five face-to-face while attending a large conference. The conference schedule was filled with government and education powerbrokers who made decisions that affected millions of Americans. The lifetime achievement award honoree was a well-known leader who had authored over twenty books used around the world. Called to the stage, he said a few comments and finished with a nod and a thank you. While clutching the wooden plaque with a gold sign loosely attached by two screws, he moved offstage to a standing ovation.

That's it? I thought. *A plaque hastily made in a local trophy shop is the pinnacle moment of recognition? Decades of labor and love, all for a moment's standing ovation? There has to be more, doesn't there?* I looked around the room at the thousands of people and tried to read their faces, looking at their reactions. This was the highest public recognition at the convention, and yet it didn't seem like enough to me.

My eyes widened as I recognized within me a roaring drive for even more of others' approval and applause. In that moment I wanted something *more* than to speak, write books, and develop future leaders—or a plaque. I recognized the desire for prominence over that of faithful and effective service to Jesus. I wanted to be king of whatever jungle I was in. It was temptation's call to pursue *greater* recognition. Those who have a drive for success know this feeling. The conference exposed that I had moved my focus toward achievement for others' applause rather than being satisfied with work I did in obedience of Jesus.

I'm no longer surprised or bothered when I meet someone at a conference struggling with the same thing. Those conversations include questions on how to write, speak, and develop their platform. The request is familiar and comes from an admirable desire to make an impact. But also hidden within can be a desire to be recognized and valued. It says we need to do ministry *and* be known as doing well, maybe even to be seen as one of the best. It says we need to follow Jesus *and* be recognized by others as exemplary.

The truth is that we will never be prominent enough to satisfy this longing. If our goal is to be big, we'll never be big enough. We may get some applause for a short run, but the allure of recognition will taunt us and lead us farther back into the wilds and away from our original path. That desire stalks our heart until we confess—or are consumed. It's too easy to trade obedience to the One for trinkets, awards made of wood or glass. When our days are over, another person will readily take our place and easily do just as well or better. And our plaques will end up at Goodwill or in a grandchild's attic.

Gordon Smith notes that we need to sustain a "holy indifference" to the temptation to prominence: honor, careerism, or reputation.[2] Ego among God's leaders is nothing new. The disciples argued who would be greatest in the kingdom. As the disciples and others were heading to Jerusalem, Jesus told them about his impending death. James and John's mom grabbed her sons and brought them to Jesus, asking that they be honored in his coming kingdom (Mt 20:20-28). The other disciples heard the conversation and were indignant. Jesus summoned them and said that "me first" and "lording it over others" were the ways of the world. He then instructed, "But among you it will be different" (Mt 20:26 NLT).

The disciples still didn't get it. Just a few days later, at their last supper together before Jesus' arrest, the disciples again argued about who would be greatest among them (Lk 22:24). Jesus repeated his speech that in God's kingdom "greatness" is measured differently than outside of his kingdom (Lk 22:25-26; see Lk 9:23).

HOLDING ON TO CONTROL

Brenda leads a residence-focused ministry for college students. She gained the attention of the ministry leadership while on a short-term mission trip where her strong leadership skills and positive spirit held the team together during adversity. After hiring Brenda, the leaders were perplexed that the residence was experiencing a surprising amount of turmoil. The college students resented Brenda, even avoiding her.

SELF-CHECK

There is a list of yes-no questions used by counselors who work with Christian leaders, including pastors, to help diagnose issues related to prominence.[a] These are uncomfortable to answer, but this temptation requires our best effort to drag it out of our blind spot:

1. Do you feel like you're indispensable to your organization or business? Are you more so than others around you?

2. Do you expect to receive recognition from others for your work?

3. Do you exaggerate about your achievements and talents?

4. Do you think about being successful, powerful, or even beautiful to others?

5. Do you think that only those who are equal or better than you can understand you and your situation?

6. As a leader, do you assume unquestioning compliance with your expectations?

7. Are you willing to take advantage of others or manipulate others to get the decisions and actions that you want?

8. Do you find yourself envious of others or believe that others are envious of you?

9. Would those around you say that you behave in an arrogant manner sometimes?

10. Do you think you're invulnerable to any of the previous nine?

This is a challenging list. If a Christian leader answers no to question 10, do you think they are in danger in anyway? These temptations require our greatest awareness and wisdom, and probably a conversation partner to help us spot the panting for prominence along the path toward "success" in ministry.

---

[a]Surprisingly, Christian counselors have told me that narcissistic personality disorder is more of an issue among Christian leaders than we might guess. This list is modified from Mayo Clinic materials. See "Narcissistic Personality Disorder," *Mayo Clinic*, accessed June 6, 2016, www.mayoclinic.org/diseases-conditions/narcissistic-personality-disorder/basics/symptoms/con-20025568.

Upon closer inspection Brenda's drive and strong personality had created a performance-based culture (more common in Christian ministries than we want to admit). She would get upset if students missed one of her events or were overly talkative during meetings. The expectations, rules, and guidelines drowned out any whisper of grace. Brenda seemed to have forgotten that many of her students were heavily involved in extracurricular activities, the very thing that had given Brenda an opportunity to grow. Brenda had forgotten her own story, and that ministry takes place in the middle of life's realities.

Control is largely about power, not leadership. Parker Palmer says, "The power that tempts us is never power with or for others, but always power *over* something or someone."[3] Mike Myatt says that the attempt to lead through control is the most common mistake leaders make: "Leaders simply operate at their best when they understand their ability to influence is much more fruitful than their ability to control."[4] He says that control restricts potential, limits initiative, and inhibits talent. Yet it's still a widely used approach in Christian circles and unfortunately is allowed to persist more than it should.

> One indication of a leader's openness is to see if they are a good follower too. Following others well requires maturity and humility.

One indication of a leader's openness is to see if they are a good follower too. Following others well requires maturity and humility.

Jesus told his listeners to take up their cross *daily* (Lk 9:23). He knew what we've seen in practice: following Christ requires the regular practice of surrender, giving up control. It's a walk that takes a "not my will, but yours be done" posture.

BE AWARE

How can you tell if the temptation of holding on to control is stalking you? Consider the following questions and action steps:

1. How do you feel when someone else is in charge? Of you? Do you work for their success or rejoice in their struggles? Practice working behind the scenes with the leader to help them succeed.

2. When you read John's words that Christ must become greater and he (John) must become less, do you start thinking about how hard that would be (Jn 3:30)? Practice not seizing God's glory. When you are asked for advice or answers, wait five seconds before answering and pray, "Your will, God, not mine." Then answer.

3. When you read about Brenda's leadership situation, do you think first about the flexibility that the students need, or do you think about how hard it must be for Brenda to maintain order in a residence situation? Make a plan to practice attending to the needs of a group you are leading rather than forcing an agenda.

4. If I suggested that you pray a prayer of surrender ("God, this is your day") how would you react if God actually did exercise his control in unanticipated ways? Practice praying it three times a day for a week.

VALUING SHINY STUFF

Since I played sports year-round in high school, the only job that fit into my schedule was delivering the morning newspaper. Once a month I'd have to collect money door-to-door, and it was the least fun part of the job. After a few stops I'd make my way down to Groom's Drug Store with my bank bag of money. I was after a hot caramel sundae topped with two bags of Planter's peanuts. During collection week I'd end up at Groom's almost every day, and

I'd also buy a few packs of baseball cards during each visit. Newspaper delivery boys didn't make much money to begin with, and those with a taste for ice cream who loved baseball ended up with even less. But I believed that ice cream and baseball cards would make me feel better.

Over time the caramel sundaes were replaced with music, which gave way to electronics and all sorts of hobbies, clothing, and now books. Amazon and other online retailers taunt me each month with the temptation that if I had *that*, then I'd feel better. Perhaps something else triggers your impulse, the shiny "Buy Me" sign catching the corner of your eye or the latest picture you spotted on Pinterest. Unfortunately, like the caramel sundaes of old, we soon discover that the value of "stuff" eventually fades and is pushed aside by newer and shinier stuff.

I'm not alone in this discovering that shiny stuff doesn't satisfy or improve our lives. For decades research has shown there is a negative relationship between happiness and materialism. The greater the materialism, the greater the unhappiness. And the greater the chance is for psychological illness.[5] You will rarely hear that anywhere. We swim in a culture of consumerism and are often unable to see that our pursuit of "bigger, better, and best" is a never-satisfied desire that may consume us.

No one talks about greed much anymore. In fact, we idolize it in our magazines and on TV. We certainly don't often speak of greed in Christian circles, yet it can devour a Christian leader as fast as any of the big five. Spiritual leaders have not been able to master their material appetites and heed the proverb "Don't wear yourself out trying to get rich. / Be wise enough to know when to quit" (Prov 23:4 NLT). Shiny stuff deceives us by suggesting we will be happier, more complete, or more successful. It's an illusion. Our affections expose our greed: "Though your riches increase, /

do not set your heart on them" (Ps 62:10). I've seen too many young workers, even those with adequate salaries, toss aside their calling and choose to pursue more. It's not that they went to pursue God's call in another line of work; they left because they want to have *more*.

> True godliness with contentment is itself great wealth. After all, we brought nothing with us when we came into the world, and we can't take anything with us when we leave it. So if we have enough food and clothing, let us be content.
>
> But people who long to be rich fall into temptation and are trapped by many foolish and harmful desires that plunge them into ruin and destruction. (I Tim 6:6-9 NLT)

Contentedness is easier to write about than to possess, especially for achievement-oriented types like many leaders. Christian leaders of the past understood that when we set out to follow Christ, we must leave behind our desires and be content with what God

SELF-CHECK

Consider the following questions and actions to assess your susceptibility to the temptation of shiny stuff:

1. Don't purchase anything for a week. You may want to stock up on groceries and gasoline before the week starts. In the course of that week you may discover how often you purchased things out of habit or to feel better.

2. Imagine Jesus said to you what he said to the rich young leader: "Give all that you have to the poor." Could you do that? What are the limits you would put on that kind of action?

3. Some people have to have the newest smartphone as soon as it is released. Some people need the newest game or clothes. What do you have to have as soon as it's available? Can you explain why to your mentor or supervisor?

provides. Paul learned that the secret of being content was Christ, regardless of how much or how little he had. St. Anthony said that demons used to "coax" him with gold. We now travel *to* places where gold, silver, and the latest gadgets sparkle. Are we even aware of such coaxing in our current consumerist culture full of advertising?

PURSUING INAPPROPRIATE INTIMACY

God's gift of sexuality is arguably our most vulnerable area of temptation. History and Scripture have shown that no one is immune to the temptation and charms of lust masquerading as intimacy. Despite the vast coverage and attention given to it, sexual misconduct remains a significant problem for men and women in ministry.[6] Most people fall prey because they ignore the warnings from within, from others, and from God's Word. They justify flirting and inappropriate fascination and actions. They have stepped out of the safety zone and too close to the edge. If sexual sin can ensnare King David, a young man eventually described as after God's own heart (1 Sam 13:14), it can happen to any man or woman. And yet there are ways through this temptation.

Those who engage in private sexual misconduct deceive themselves into thinking it will never be discovered. I've known men involved in highly structured accountability groups who later were found to be engaged in extramarital affairs during those same years. As a pastor I've done too many interventions in which pornography, affairs, and sexual misconduct were exposed. The level of resignation, embarrassment, and remorse among those caught in the snares of sexual temptation are among the deepest I've witnessed in Christian ministry.

At the same time, as is always the case with Jesus, the most dramatic examples I've seen of God's grace, forgiveness, and restoration in ministry have been the lives of those who have fallen to sexual sin, who repented and engaged in a restoration process with others, and then allowed the Holy Spirit to lead them forward as a new person (2 Cor 5:17). Certainly, the consequences endured, but, like the woman caught in adultery, those once ensnared experienced firsthand what it was like to hear Jesus' words "Neither do I condemn you. . . . Go now and leave your life of sin" (Jn 8:1-11).

How do we avoid temptation in a sexually saturated culture? What safeguards can we put in place to protect our family, our work, and ourselves? Clearly, there were early warning signs for the Christian leaders who have fallen to sexual temptations. Ignoring these signs allowed desire to leap out and drag them away. I want to focus on three of the most common areas where leaders get in trouble.

If you're experiencing sexual temptation or are involved in private sexual misconduct, this information is worthy of your immediate attention. For example, viewing pornography can be a gateway to riskier sexual decisions. The beast has its claws in your flesh and is slowly dragging you into the brush. If this is your experience and you're afraid of what might happen if someone discovered what's been going on, you'll be surprised how helpful, supportive, and discreet good Christian counselors are. If you don't know of any, ask others and I am sure they can point you to someone who can help.[7]

Flirting. Kathy and Brad had worked together in the ministry for two years before the affair happened. Brad was single and Kathy was divorced with two kids. In difficult conversations they had with the other staff members before they left, both pointed to flirtatious conversations in the office as the spark that started their attraction to one another.

I remember stopping by that office often, but I didn't notice any untoward behavior. However, I did notice that staff members often talked and teased each other about marriage and sex.

Flirtation is common among young adults. It's a language we learn in adolescence, but we need to unlearn in our adult years. Flirting starts out as a glance, comment, or touch, and grows into conversation and even extended time spent together. There's an excitement to the joking and the attention-giving that makes us feel good about ourselves. Flirting and flaunting are treated as necessary and desirable practices. They can seem harmless, but it's a bit foolish to think we can survive what others haven't. If you're a man or woman in a position of leadership, you need to understand your position of power and the impact that has on those of the opposite gender, especially those who are drawn to power and influence.

What kind of person captures your attention? Who treats you in a way that makes you feel special and makes you smile? Flirting is easy to spot in others, but less so in ourselves. It's made evident in the extra glance, the long stare, the bright-eyed smile, the joking, and being in close proximity. When you see yourself drawn to another, be guarded, take a step back, distance yourself from the other while drawing closer to God, and take the scary but helpful step to tell someone you trust.

For those who are married, sometimes the vulnerability arises when the marital relationship is not healthy to begin with. When one spouse is in ministry, they can devote so much time, attention, and affection to their calling that it creates problems and jealousies with the other spouse. These can't be ignored; the family is an area of ministry that must be managed with grace and love (1 Tim 3:12-13). For most young couples this requires a new level of honesty and then selfless adjustments.

Thoughts. Imagine that one day we could start hearing each other's thoughts. Maybe it would be something like this: Turner walked into the weekly ministry staff meeting half asleep, his usual

SELF-CHECK: FIVE WAYS TO BUILD PERSONAL SAFEGUARDS

1. Always be able to account for your time.
2. Be conscious of when and where you're alone with someone of the opposite gender.
3. Make all computers, smartphones, and social media accounts available to your spouse or a godly friend.
4. Watch what you watch. Sensitivities can be numbed and norms redefined by constant viewing of sexually explicit media.
5. Talk about your temptations with a Christian counselor. Instead of being hunted by temptations, go on a hunt for healing. Let the Holy Spirit do a new work in your life.

Thursday morning demeanor, and shuffled to his seat at the end of the long conference table.

"Ha, Turner's got his usual half gallon of coffee. Won't help him be any more alert."

"Wonder when Turner is going to realize there's more than fleece to wear to work?"

"Wow, I really think Turner is handsome. Too bad he's dating Sara."

"I wonder what brilliant comment Turner will make today that no one will take seriously."

Turner thought, *"I'm hearing comments but no one is speaking."*

"What? You can hear our thoughts?"

"Oh, man, I was only kidding."

"Me, too."

Our thinking is a playground, incubator, and at times a sanctuary. If people could hear our thoughts, committee meetings and teaching sessions would function very differently. We'd learn that our thinking doesn't always line up well with what we do or the impression we give to others.

Here's the thing: *Someone does hear all we are thinking.*

Those who fall from ministry due to sexual sin confess that they had been struggling with the secret thoughts for years. Their mental rehearsals created enough momentum to break through any guardedness. Jesus warned his followers about the danger, power, and sinfulness of lustful thinking: "I tell you that anyone who looks at a woman lustfully has already committed adultery with her in his heart" (Mt 5:28). James wrote, "Each person is tempted when they are dragged away by their own evil desire and enticed. Then, after desire has conceived, it gives birth to sin; and sin, when it is full-grown, gives birth to death" (Jas 1:14-15).

The struggle for our transformation begins in our minds (Rom 12:1-2). This battle must be won! It's a struggle for transformation, in which our minds, hearts and desires are renewed and thus fulfill the will of God in and through us. I see too many who try to manage their sin only to have it eventually consume them. Our thinking isn't neutral, nor can it be managed by our own will.

So what do we do? It isn't helpful to say to yourself, *Don't think about that.* Instead, say, *Think about what you know to be true. God created you, God loves you, God passionately pursues you. Think about the evidence of God's pursuit of you. Where were you five years ago? Where are you today?* In Philippians 4:8-9, Paul lays out a list of things to think about, and then offers himself as a model of how to live. Rather than getting stuck in thought loops, be transformed by following Paul's thought-renovation process.

Fascinations. When our thoughts begin to grow, they become something that holds our attention longer than it should. The Internet has become the incubator for all sorts of fascinations for us. We can find interest groups for those who collect flashlights (they exist!), for fan clubs of the latest teenage star, for people who want to make money via a blog that tells others how to make money via blogging. There are also interest groups for sexual encounters. The growth of cyber affairs is alarming. Since they start with no physical contact, they seem harmless, but they aren't. The hack of the Ashley Madison website brought to light how virtual sexual fascinations, even by Christian leaders, can grow into the pursuit of extramarital affairs.[8]

The Internet has helped turn pornography into a $13 billion business. Fifty-one percent of pastors say that pornography is a temptation, and 68 percent of all divorces happened because one person met a lover online.[9] We cannot continue to be unaware of our own actions, and we cannot be so confident to think that we'll never succumb to this temptation. If your response is *It won't happen to me*, counselors will tell you that such a response increases your vulnerability in this area.

Proverbs equates sexual fascinations to hot coals heaped into our lap; they will burn us (Prov 6:25-35). Better to address the fascinations now. Christ can forgive, redeem, and renew. But when people succumb, the embarrassment and shame they feel is painful and overwhelming. In the actions of one person, families are devastated, ministries and churches cut in two, and relationships are damaged. Guard yourself in your interactions with others and what you're thinking about, and be ruthless in dealing with any private fascinations.

Consider some questions to help you think through some aspects of temptation. When reading about flirting and fascination, did certain faces or recent memories come to mind? Did you think, *That's not flirting, we're just having fun*? If so, it may be flirting. What do your thoughts turn to when there is no one around?

RELISHING RESENTMENT

Few of us *want* to be resentful, at least I hope we don't. It's not a goal that makes too many New Year's resolution lists. Of the big five, this temptation gets the least press because it seems the least dangerous, which makes it particularly effective. It's perhaps the most common temptation and can devour us with ease. You don't need a safari tour to see bitter people in church and ministry leadership.

Years ago Andrea started attending Pastor Trevor's church. Kevin, her husband, didn't. Kevin had no time for God. As a result, prayer requests for Kevin were common at Andrea's new church. After a couple years, one Easter Sunday Kevin went to another church, heard the gospel, and decided to follow Jesus. It should have been a wonderful moment. But Kevin hadn't gone to Pastor Trevor's church that morning. And Pastor Trevor grew bitter. He questioned the reality of the conversion. He accused the other pastor of "sheep stealing." He raised enough questions that Andrea doubted Kevin's relationship with God. Eventually, there was enough tension that Andrea and Kevin divorced. All because of Pastor Trevor's resentment.

Bitterness draws us in by telling us what we deserve, pointing out the good things that others have or do in comparison, and then soothing us by pointing to others to blame for our lack. Resentment or bitterness intertwines itself in our circumstances (Ruth 1:20; 1 Sam 30:6; Job 10:1; 21:25; Prov 17:25; Jer 6:26), a root that produces some smelly flowers (Heb 12:15). The Greek word for bitterness originates in "sharp" or "pointed." Bitterness is marked by resentment and jealousy, thoughts that what we have is insufficient and that we should have the blessings of others. Bitterness doesn't really help, but it entices us into thinking it will make us feel better. We drink it in like poison and then wait for the other to get sick—all the while we experience its debilitating effects. Bitterness is a particularly devastating sin (Acts 8:23) that comes from a sinful heart (Rom 3:9-14), and it grieves the Holy Spirit (Eph 4:30-31). It has no place in the lives of those who have surrendered their will and future to God.

Fortunately, bitterness has a tranquilizer in forgiveness. The stories of Esau and Jacob (Gen 33:1-11) and the prodigal son (Lk 15:25-32) highlight the role that God-honoring forgiveness plays in overcoming bitterness. Paul lays it out plainly, "Get rid of all bitterness, rage and anger, brawling and slander, along with every form of malice. Be kind and compassionate to one another, forgiving each other, just as in Christ God forgave you" (Eph 4:30-31).

I want to go back to Andrea and Kevin, the couple who divorced. God worked in the lives of Andrea and Kevin, bringing healing and eventually remarriage. God is able to overcome the damage we do to those affected by our sin. But how much better would it be to never have caused the damage?

If reactions are a key to self-awareness, complaining might be a reactive practice that reveals something else is going on. Whenever you hear yourself complain, snap a mental selfie and later spend time in reflective prayer about it. What is the desire that fuels that response? Of the five desires, complaints may be the clearest teachers because they are like fast elevators to the heart, revealing what's deeper within.

SELF-CHECK

Here are some questions to help you explore how you are doing with this temptation:

1. To what level is there dissatisfaction in your life?

2. Can you identify others who seem to be getting better opportunities than you? Do you feel that they are liked better by some folks?

3. Are there times when you're sarcastic, too sharp in your speech, or that you've been complaining more than you should?

4. Is there a general level of grumpiness in your life that wasn't there a few years ago?

5. Would those around you agree with your answer to the previous question?

It's important for every Christian worker to have a season of Christian counseling in their late twenties or early thirties. Our desires and patterns seem to become clear during these years, and it's important to work through these with a godly counselor. Think of it as a twenty-thousand-mile checkup or a five-year physical. It will help you avoid some potential problems and pain, and to realize greater spiritual, relational, and leadership health.

A HOPEFUL FUTURE

It may be easy to dismiss this chapter as being full of issues you are not struggling with. *The big five won't get me, will they?* From the time I started writing this chapter until right now, several friends have been consumed by or drawn away from their positions by one of the big five. In fact, if I listed what had happened, you'd be shocked. I've been shocked! But it's spurred me on to put these weighty matters out there for all of us to see. The big five are lying in wait for us.

There's a long list of people formerly in ministry who thought they could manage some secret, but they found that wild things can't be tamed. Do you think that they felt like exceptions to the rule, immune to the downfalls others had experienced? Do you think they were surprised when it all fell apart? Christian leader and author Joe Stowell comments:

> I have rarely seen a leader fail because they are not gifted to lead. Most often a leader fails because at some point he or she has ceased to live and lead as a follower of Christ. Leaders take the first steps toward failure when they assume they are smart enough or skilled enough to succeed at what they do on their own. Guided by their own instincts and tempted by seductive opportunities, they turn their backs on Jesus, compromise their integrity, and are taken down by the belief that they are above the rules. Or they believe the lie that they are clever enough to avoid getting caught.[10]

Before we look for a change in life and ministry, let's consider that God may want to change us. Before we take a turn that will destroy so much, let's pursue renewal and reconstruction. Before we act in selfish ways, let's again consider Christ and his sacrificial model of love, which invites us to trust him. If you're facing a tempting turn, take it to others in a trusted Christ-centered community. Start with, "This is how I'm feeling (or acting); can you help me work through this?"

Most of this chapter discusses dangers. But I want to end on a note of hope. There are many people who have *not* lost their ministry effectiveness. They were tempted, that's clear. But they were willing to open their hearts and lives to God for examination. They were willing to confront the temptation at the beginning, before it gave birth to sin. They were willing to stay away from the things that tempted them. They were willing to do the things that gave them life. They were willing to practice the obedience that I've talked about in this chapter.

Because I've watched so many people, including me, struggle with these temptations, I want to tell you that I'm praying for you. It doesn't seem very personal to do since we've likely never met. But it grows out of my pastor's heart. My life is committed to helping others lead ministry well, so I am praying regularly for readers of this book because I know that some of these steps forward are difficult and will require of us courage, humility, and new habits.

FOR GREATER AWARENESS

1. What are good ministry desires? How can you stay focused on these good desires while thwarting the not-so-desirable desires?

2. As you read through the chapter, which of the five areas of temptation seemed particularly irrelevant to you? Is it possible that you may want to avoid conversation about that subject? Go

back to it and read it again. Consider whether you are resisting God's nudging.

3. Which of the five temptations did you recognize as the most tempting? What steps have you taken to stay vigilant to its pull?

4. Have you ever sat with a godly licensed counselor or a spiritual director to talk through various areas of your life? If so, what were the outcomes from those conversations? If not, how might you benefit from a few meetings with one?

5. If you haven't yet, please take the Enneagram test if possible. Though not as accurate, there is a free version at www.9types .com/rheti/index.php. After taking it, what did you learn? What was affirmed? What was surprising? What areas of temptation does your type usually struggle with?

5

I VIVIDLY REMEMBER MY FIRST ROLLER COASTER RIDE, the Comet at Hershey Park, Pennsylvania. I was a middle school mix of nerves and excitement as we clicked our way up the first big hill. Anticipation built for what was about to happen; my grip around the metal bar tightened. We inched over the top, the hesitation prolonging the anxiety. Then we plummeted down the incline. I was sure it was straight down (though it was only 47 degrees). We shot up the next hill, my head bowing under the centrifugal force, curved around turns, dropped again, and vaulted over smaller hills before arriving at the station. My cousin and I laughed and cheered; a roller coaster junkie had been born. Let's ride again!

Sounds a bit like life in ministry, doesn't it? Ministry produces a mishmash of soaring highs and deep valleys. We nervously enter the lives of others, an often-jittery first step followed by an exhilarating drop into a new community of people. We then navigate the ups and downs, twists and turns that come at us with sometimes startling speed. One day we'll have a fruitful conversation and launch upward with confidence. The next day an event doesn't go well or we're criticized, and we feel bumped, bruised, and disoriented. We are pressed low, desperate before God, and then we are in the middle of mountain-top moments of ministry. We twist and turn in the give and take of close working relationships, and we corkscrew through private emotions that leave us dizzy and occasionally feeling upside down.

Yet we are drawn to Christian work and we love it. Let's ride again!

But this emotional ride has a risk. Our highs and lows may come at the expense of others. Our euphoria and devastation can affect our families. We can become addicted to the rush and sprint from one ministry situation to another. All the while ignoring our hearts.

THE MOST COMMON BLIND
SPOT THAT FEW DISCUSS

The emotional side of life is one of the most common areas leaders and their supervisors tend to ignore—to their own detriment. It's also the area where people problems exist, the kind that others have difficulty talking to us about.

How do we notice and handle our emotions? Those who develop and supervise others in ministry will tell you that emotional maturity will make or, in its absence, break a leader's success in ministry. Gordon Smith argues that emotional maturity should be a central concern for Christians: "We do not mature in our Christian experience unless we mature emotionally. What happens to us emotionally is not peripheral but central to our religious experience. To put it bluntly, people who are out of touch with their emotions are out of touch with God, for God speaks to us through the ebb and flow of our emotional life."[1]

The affective (or emotional) domain is part of our created identity in the image of God, a God who is described in the Bible as sometimes angry (Ps 7:11), always compassionate (Ps 86:15), persistently loving (1 Jn 4:8), joyful (Is 62:5), and at times sorrowful (Mt 26:38). When we see Jesus, fully God and human, we are taught that emotion isn't wrong or unspiritual. Jesus was tired, frustrated, and moved with compassion and affection. He grew angry; he was delighted. God reveals himself in Scripture with personality in dynamic relationship with his creation. It's assuring to know that, no matter our wiring, our personality's origin is found in God. He doesn't love only the extroverts or the punctual; he also created task-oriented introverts and those who are habitually late.

Emotions don't make something true, but they point the way to truthful matters. Luke describes a story in which a Pharisee invited Jesus to dinner and started to squirm at the outpouring of emotion by "a woman." She came to the Pharisee's house and stood behind Jesus as he reclined on the floor. She sobbed, and her tears fell on Jesus' feet, and she wiped his dirty, unwashed feet with her hair. Imagine the scene! We know of no conversation except that she was so overcome in the presence of Jesus that she *repeatedly* kissed his feet and poured perfumed oil on them (Lk 7:36-50). Simon the Pharisee wrinkled his nose and muttered at the emotional recklessness he observed. Jesus corrected Simon's thinking by pointing how he had performed none of the common courtesies (for example, water for washing his feet), yet she had shown great love for the Messiah and taken care of him at personal sacrifice in meaningful ways.

We can learn from the contrasting reactions of the Pharisee and the woman. If we care about something, then our affections are involved. For instance, we feel indignant when we see wrongs being done. We feel jubilant when we (or others) have success. We get angry when we're unable to do something, and we are sad when we face disappointment. Our emotions are not the end but an indicator that something else is going on. The Pharisee's indifference to his guest revealed his level of respect and interest in Jesus.

We witness emotional outpourings every day: joy, anger, tears, or compassion. When we see raw emotion, we know that we're witnessing something deeper than the norm, something behind the veneer we too often see. Feelings often reveal what is intensely personal and held deep within. When we can't see any emotion, we begin to question whether someone is being genuine. Ignatius said that feelings are indicators of God's work in our lives, and we benefit when we give attention "to the media of God's influence in our lives."[2]

The goal for those of us in ministry is to mature in Christlikeness emotionally, interpersonally, and intrapersonally. We want to be able to get along well with others, participate consistently well in a church community, and even relate well to others in ministry. One prominent Christian leader told me, "Those who do not work on emotional self-awareness and fluency in their twenties often become unfit for ministry in their thirties and forties."[3]

HOW TO GROW IN EMOTIONAL MATURITY

Maturity doesn't happen suddenly. It grows. Fields can grow crops without attention, but they will also grow weeds. They will be full of rocks that stunt growth and will lack the nutrients that foster growth. Farmers are intentional about enhancing the growth process. I've noticed seven ways that we can intentionally help ourselves and others grow toward emotional maturity. If we ignore our emotions and responses, seeing them as irrelevant, we will miss the chance to grow in maturity and Christlikeness. Consider these steps to help nurture the right kind of emotional crop.

1. Assign a sentry at the door. You may know the proverb "Above all else, guard your heart, / for everything you do flows from it"

(Prov 4:23). The Hebrew word for "guard" (*mishmar*) means to keep watch, to be diligent, and to protect. It may be best translated "keep watch." When a sentry was assigned to the door of city, he was to not only keep the enemy away but to allow in those who had rights to passage. To grow emotionally, we need to be open to what God wants to do in our life and cautious about other sources for how to feel and what to value.

2. Label what you feel. Mark was a successful associate pastor at a small church, and he possessed an unusual knack for being well organized. He led denominational camps and regional conferences with ease and seemed to possess an endless capacity for getting things done and done right. He was intensely driven to be successful, yet he acted in inappropriate ways within the confines of the local church. Though outwardly he appeared well-adjusted, there was a private emotional struggle churning, a wrestling match that exacerbated other suppressed problems.

On most days Mark was engaged and productive, his gifts being used to their fullest in the ministry. He felt alive. He was soaring. Then someone would say something to him or give an opportunity to another person, and Mark would be crushed. On those days he would post on social media that he wanted to quit, his default response to things when his emotional circuits would overload. Mark's emotional roller coaster went on for two years. The first part of the counselor's work with Mark was to help him recognize and label his emotions so he could take healthy steps toward healing. It's difficult to rid yourself of anger (through the work of Christ) if you don't recognize you're angry. No one had ever helped Mark see when he was angry, sad, or hurt. He didn't want to admit any of it, and no one had ever taught him that, with God's forgiveness and restoration, he could have control of those responses.

3. Be aware of others' emotions. Though an enormously gifted leader, Monica wasn't aware of others' emotions, and people were often frustrated by her. She gave off an unintended vibe of superiority and entitlement. Mix in her strong task orientation, and Monica had little problem saying whatever came to her mind as she worked with others, completely unaware of how the comments affected them and how others felt about her. If she paid attention, her reactions would have helped her see pride's role in her thinking. As it was, her supervisor didn't step in, and soon her volunteer role was taken from her and she was left wondering what happened.

4. Identify the intensity of your feelings. I was irritated most of the day today. An early morning email from a student's parent put me in a bad mood. And it carried into the rest of my conversations. The student wanted to participate in a project I was coordinating and did not communicate it well to his folks, who then responded negatively to an incomplete set of information. I addressed it easily, but my internal irritation persisted into the afternoon.

Kelly asked me why it bothered me so much. (She majored in psychology, so she asks such questions.) I had already recognized the unusual strength of my response, and I knew that the parent's email had triggered a memory for me. Once I identified the source and intensity, I was able to step away and not make the student's situation be about me. He ended up participating and everything went amazingly well. But if I would've reacted quickly with the family, it would've been a different story. Noticing the unusual intensity of my reaction helped me to not overreact and ruin a ministry moment.

5. Manage your emotions. Christian leaders must first learn to manage their emotions and then to be led by the Spirit instead of by their feelings. "Be very careful, then, how you live—not as unwise but as wise, making the most of every opportunity, because the days are evil. Therefore do not be foolish, but understand what the Lord's will is. Do not get drunk on wine, which leads to debauchery. Instead, be filled with the Spirit" (Eph 5:15-18).

In his letter to the Galatians, Paul listed the acts of the "flesh" (Gal 5:19-21). These emotional qualities are in stark contrast to his list of the fruit of the Spirit a few verses later (vv. 22-23). Peter, who knew a few things about the need for and the danger of emotional outbursts, echoed the need for careful attention in light of the spiritual battle we are in: "Be alert and of sober mind. Your enemy the devil prowls around like a roaring lion looking for someone to devour. Resist him, standing firm in the faith, because you know that the family of believers throughout the world is undergoing the same kind of sufferings" (1 Pet 5:8-9).

6. Learn from your emotions. As you interact with God and others, you will have emotional responses. When appropriate, consider the underlying cause to what you're feeling. Are these emotions telling you the truth or deceiving you in some way? Might God be stirring in you something new? In what ways might your feelings be masking something important? Is your emotional reaction appropriate to what happened? What does your response to your emotions say about you? What might they suggest about your spiritual life?

7. Submit your emotions to Jesus. We are called to love God with our heart, soul, mind, and strength. It's easy to imagine how we can love God with our strength. It's even easier to see how we can love God with our soul. But how can we love God with our emotions? Is it possible to offer our joy and grief and anxiousness and anger and relief to God?

I think it is. When we do, our conversations with God will be something like this: "Is this something that makes you angry too? Am I rejoicing as much as you are? Would you help me be less anxious about disappointing you?" As we learn to measure our emotional responses against the model and teachings of Jesus, we will grow.

SELF-CHECK: HOW TO GROW IN EMOTIONAL MATURITY

- Assign a sentry. Pray for what God wants to do in your life. Developing character includes being guarded.

- Take an inventory. There are many good resources at the Emotionally Healthy Spirituality website (emotionally healthy.org), including a helpful personal assessment.

- Observe and identify emotions in yourself and in others. Keep a journal or talk about them in conversation. Ask a trusted friend, "What do you experience when you're around me?"

- Analyze situations and look for the underlying feelings or emotions that were present. The most practical way I've learned to do this in the moment is simply to talk less and listen more. Look for emotional clues in nonverbal responses and in word choices.

- Seek to understand the *why* behind your emotions and reactions, especially within your context. When you find a *why* question you can't answer or a wound you can't seem to heal on your own, seek out a Christian therapist to work on that issue. Like a world-class athlete needs skilled physical trainers, ministry leaders need skilled emotional help during seasons of their lives.

- Reflect on your relationships for emotional content, for opportunities to model emotional maturity, and for potential points of conflict.

THE COMMON EMOTIONAL STATES

I'd like to briefly touch on a few of the frequent emotional states that we experience. Though I could identify more, these four are familiar to those who have traveled on the roller-coaster ministry track.

Joy. When Aaron answered the phone, the caller identified herself as a representative of the Indianapolis Colts. Aaron was skeptical, thinking that his own practical jokes had prompted a return volley. After a few seconds of conversation, he realized it was legitimate and that he had been selected as the Colt's "super fan." His reaction was the epitome of what it means to be "overjoyed." The Colts were sending him to the Super Bowl! The super fan designation was accurate because Aaron knows no middle ground when it comes to being a sports fan.

We all know sports fans like Aaron, right? The outcome of each day's game may affect their mood, but deep down, regardless of losing streaks, their affection is unquestioned. Emotions come and go (what had been a common experience for Chicago Cubs fans), but point the way toward deeper affection and its causes. I start this conversation about common affections with joy because it is such a consistent descriptor in Scripture of a mature Christian life.

The goal of the Christian faith is to experience Christ's presence in such a way that his "joy may be in you and that your joy may be complete" (Jn 15:11). It's what Jesus wanted for his disciples. It's what Paul desired for those he wrote his pastoral letters to. Joy is deeply rooted in our hearts. It's a quality that can be present even in the midst of suffering and persecution.

I am convinced that at the intersection of maturity, Christ-centeredness, and contentedness, we find joy. Its presence or absence is telling. When we are joyful, we have no anxiety, fear, need for control, and anger. When there is joy, there is freedom and confidence. When we see people who are joyful in spite of difficult circumstances, we take notice. When joy is present, maturity and spiritual depth are right behind.

A few years back I went through a long period of what seemed like joylessness. Though I'm not sure anyone around me (but Kelly) could guess that I was experiencing it, each work-related day was spent putting one foot in front of the other and making it through to the next. I wasn't depressed or down, but each day had no flavor. The ministry was going and growing well, and people were pleased. I just couldn't click my heels to get out of it, and my spiritual retreats and devotional life did not fix the problem. It was a "dark night of the soul" period.

After researching the topic and hearing the stories of others who had similar periods, I addressed three things. First, I persisted in my devotional practices. The purpose was not to fix myself emotionally but rather to draw close to God, a subtle but important distinction. A common problem with joylessness is that we've taken our primary focus off of God and onto ourselves. Second, I intentionally developed godly friendships. We too often withdraw when just the opposite is needed. Godly friendships have a Spirit-infused power that eradicate all sorts of protective struggles. Third, I assigned a sentry to see what was really going on and what God had for me. Especially in ministry during times of discontent, attention is essential.

Sometimes we go through emotional flatness, deep valleys of despair, and discontent, but a "dark night of the soul" is an opportunity to ask the deeper questions we've ignored. It's too easy to give up. Unless we are confident that God is using the discontent to call us to something else, we must hang in there.

In that period of what I characterize as joylessness, I discovered that my emotional disposition was a product of a growth plateau, my personality, and some self-centered restlessness. The latter was tied to a creative dissatisfaction with routine. I began to pray a short prayer each day: "Dear God, what I have is enough. Thank you." I wanted to be joyful for what is rather than what wasn't. Over those eight months, I think God fashioned a new level of maturity within me, one that has produced a deeper joy in Christ than ever.

What makes you joyful in life? What makes you rejoice in your ministry? Spend some time looking back over the last few months. Jot down a list of the moments when you recognized the presence of joy in your life. What was happening? How was God working? What surprises you about the joy at those moments? And think through the three disciplines I discovered helpful in my own recognition of joy. How intimate is your relationship to Christ right now? Are you moving toward or away from godly relationships? Are you committed to obedience or seeking good feelings? This time of reflection may help you rediscover the joy of working with God in his ministry.

Fear. We've grown up in a media culture that fuels our fears and those of the people we want to lead. Cable news channels use fear to motivate us to watch for hourly updates. Companies use fear to get us to purchase their products. Politicians use fear of the other candidate to motivate the public to vote for them. Religious leaders sometimes use fear to elicit conformity and help sell books or teach seminars. And sometimes our fears bubble up from deep within.

Kary Oberbrunner says that sometimes our fears can be traced back to our past hurts. In his book *The Deeper Path*, he says that in order for us to heal we are going to have to excavate and confront our fears—of change, failure, and success.[4] He says that we avoid change because we crave control, and when we change we feel we've left a bit of ourselves behind. He adds that life is change, and we can either ignore it or invite it, but it will always show up.

Oberbrunner observes that these fears keep some of us from trying to accomplish things. "Truth is we will fail, it's part of life. But be encouraged: fear means we're moving, growing, and exploring. The alternative is never trying, a clear indication we're dead."[5] He acknowledges that it's strange to think of success as a source of fear, but some of us don't want the spotlight. It scares us.

We're comfortable avoiding the scrutiny that comes with success, that people might discover the real us, seeing our pain and weaknesses, and discover our limitations.

Here's what Jesus did to help his disciples with the fear of failure. In Matthew 10, he's sending the Twelve out in teams of two. He tells them where to go and what to say. And then he says, "If anyone will not welcome you or listen to your words," leave that place (v. 14). Jesus lets them know that people will reject them, and this isn't failure. He talks about being taken to court, and this isn't failure. He says that people will hate them because they hate him, and this isn't failure.

The failure would be to not go where he sends them.

God tells us story after story of people who didn't go, at least not right away. Jonah, Peter, John Mark, David, Gideon, and Moses are all people who didn't go right away. And Jesus, aware of how humans are, asks which of two sons honored his father's will to work in a vineyard: Was it the one who refused at first and then went, or the one who said he would go but didn't? And the answer, simply, is the one who finally obeyed (Mt 21:28-32). God works with fearful people who are willing to take steps to follow him, even in the face of internal fears.

Anxiety. One recent summer I suddenly experienced anxiety. I don't know exactly what triggered it, but I was afraid and bound up by the unknown. I was anxious about my work, about Kelly's new business career, whether the sump pump would go out, and even whether I'd have enough resources for retirement. Whatever came into my mind, I was anxious about it, and I didn't know why.

As I began talking about it with Christian leaders older than me, I discovered that anxiety is more common in leadership than we know. It turns out that those with a strong drive or persistent insecurities often struggle with anxiety. Anxiety has become one of the top psychological disorders today. It affects Christians, people who are mid-career, and is especially prominent among adolescents. We know one of the signs of a mature faith is a decline in anxiety and an increase in peace, which makes some of us worry even more about not measuring up because we're so anxious!

Anxiety presents rich opportunities for spiritual discernment if we are willing to seek help from God and others. In its common forms, anxiety lies at the edge of trust, pulling us away from seeing and living in the world as God intends. Satan's goal is to bring us to the point of despair where we feel like there is no going back. Anxiety is a thief, stealing us of perspective and dragging us down.

The steps away from anxiety are also those mentioned before. We do not abandon our spiritual practices, even if they seem inert or stale. We need to move toward, not away from, Christian community. We recognize anxiety's patterns in our lives, confess any related sins the Spirit reveals, and then move forward, knowing that it will not devour us.

> Do not be anxious about anything, but in every situation, by prayer and petition, with thanksgiving, present your requests to God. And the peace of God, which transcends all understanding, will guard your hearts and your minds in Christ Jesus. (Phil 4:6-7)

Anger. I'm amazed how quickly anger can pop up in life. We can experience the love of the Creator, minister to his people with grace and kindness, and yet be very angry with his world. We can experience a seemingly fantastic church service on Sunday and be mad an hour later at the teenage waiter who brought us a Diet Coke with lemon instead of a regular Coke with a lime. I can read Psalm 103, experience deep gratitude for God, and yet be intensely angry at the family pet five minutes later. And don't get me started about how some of us react while driving.

Our angry responses to the world are one of the easiest to spot. The loud explosion of words and actions are hard to hide. But the brief storm can create emotional messes that take hours or years to clean up. As Proverbs says, "An angry person stirs up conflict, / and a hot-tempered person commits many sins" (Prov 29:22).

Anger is often the result of unresolved hurt, fear, frustration, embarrassment, or humiliation. It is often easier for a person to say they are angry than to say they are hurt, embarrassed, or humiliated. A thirteen year old will be angry when a more sophisticated emotion (scared, frustrated, or hurt) is under the surface.

Often anger is more connected to an accumulation of frustration than the size of a current offense. That's because the explosion is often held in check by sheer willpower. And most of us don't know that willpower is a finite resource. There will be an explosion of anger unless we allow ourselves to recover from suppressed anger by doing things like exercising, receiving an apology, finding agreement in the midst of conflict, or taking a Sunday afternoon nap. When we are aware that we are getting angry, we can avert the explosion by stepping back to get perspective ("an explosion now will cost me later"), finding healthy avenues of release (a short walk, a deep breath, a stretch), and constructive conversations in the relationships ("I'm sorry, I'm distracted today. Could you repeat that?").

After a frustrating event, we can learn useful lessons about ourselves by asking, *Why did that make me angry?* Asking the question can untangle subjects bound up within us over time. We need to examine why particular people cause us frustration, why certain situations leave us feeling powerless and wanting to lash out, how much rest we have been getting. We are looking for patterns, things that we can address to avoid the rapid decompression.

One place to look for the seeds of anger is in our sarcasm. I've heard that sarcasm is basically anger on simmer. Sarcastic thoughts and comments bring to light qualities like discouragement and bitterness, which would rather stay hidden and grow in dark corners. Simply put, you need to know what makes you angry. The worst anger may be suppressed, and then it pops up looking like depression or in other forms. Find out what makes you angry and seek God about the best way to handle those things, how to take the correct actions when it does happen, and how to forgive as Jesus forgave.

There is another perspective on anger, however. Some of us see righteous anger as essential to strong leadership. J. Oswald Sanders listed it as an essential quality for spiritual leaders. He noted that great leaders like William Wilberforce and Martin Luther were motivated to action by their anger at injustices they observed.[6] One time, Martin Luther King Jr. was forced to give up his seat to white passengers who had boarded the bus he was on. The bus driver was angry that King and his teacher didn't move fast enough to get up, so he made them stand for the ninety miles on a hot summer trip to King's home in Atlanta. The anger that King experienced that day served as motivation for his leadership in the civil rights movement.

King worked to channel his anger toward a higher purpose and not to become bitter or full of hatred, lashing back like those who attacked him. His steady and consistent leadership in a time when emotions boiled over repeatedly serves to this day as a model for all leaders.[7] It's more common to see anger that isn't holy or channeled well. Luther, Wilberforce, King, and others who managed it well in times of extreme adversity modeled how to be aware of anger and not let it overtake them in their actions. They let forgiveness overcome anger's temptation, a pattern exemplified repeatedly in the life of Christ.

BEING CURIOUS

Two characteristics of maturity are love and curiosity. If compassion is the mature response to others, then curiosity is the mature response to the world we live in. Think about it—a curious person assumes there is more to learn and discover, is humble, doesn't let fear or pride or other feelings inhibit them, and has the appreciation for new and beautiful things. If we work to be loving and have a sense of curious awe, it's likely that emotional health will follow. If love and curiosity are absent, then we're likely self-focused and emotionally unable to connect with others well.

Perhaps it's best if we adopt a disposition of curiosity toward the ups and downs and twists and turns of our life. Rather than seeking a lazy-river existence, perhaps we need to take a step toward real life and its wavy nature. Life and all of its trappings are opportunities for us to draw closer and deeper in love with Christ, to develop a love for God and others, and to see the Holy Spirit work in our lives as he helps us mature. In many cases it's not *that* we're experiencing the tides of emotions, but *what* we're doing in response.

FOR GREATER AWARENESS

1. If we took up sentry duty at the door of your heart, the place deep within your being, what would we observe? What would you want us to keep out? What would we welcome?

2. Did you find yourself enjoying this chapter or rushing to get through it? Did you skip over any section? Why did you have those responses to this chapter's content?

3. When was the last time you went over the edge and plummeted emotionally? What was the emotion? What did you do to find healing?

4. How authentic do you think you are? Does what you experience deep within line up with the person you appear to be to others?

5. Who is your mentor? How has this person helped you in your Christian walk? If you don't have one, are you willing to submit yourself to someone who will invest in your life to help in your walk as a Christian leader?

6. When is the last time you stopped to let your curiosity out and simply be in awe of what God has done for you? Where can you look for it?

6

DAVID LETTERMAN REVOLUTIONIZED American late-night television in the 1980s and beyond, paving the way for other late-night hosts to perform comedy sketches, stunts, and interviews outside of the studio. The silly exploits were a strange mix of interesting and lame, but each night folks would tune in to see what Dave would do for his "Top Ten List," stupid pet or human tricks, or routine with one of his cast of characters. One of Letterman's earliest stunts included seeing what would happen if he put various items under an eighty-ton press. Viewers would write in with ideas of what to crush, and he'd try the most outlandish ones. It was mesmerizing to watch what would happen, what would ooze out under the weight of the press, whether it was a watermelon or an iPhone under duress.

Ask people in Christian ministry how they're doing, and you'll often find a wearied response, a comment about stress, or a grunt. Ministry has pressures, some of which are difficult to explain or identify. Consider this list and make a check by those you have experienced:

❑ I feel pressure to be consistent in how I treat people.

❑ I feel pressure to maintain a high quality of output.

❑ I feel pressure to be knowledgeable and well read on all topics.

❑ I feel pressure to be well organized yet instantaneously available for counseling.

❑ I feel pressure to not say (or admit) I am exhausted.

❑ I feel pressure from not having enough money personally or organizationally.

❑ I feel pressure to measure up to expectations of my family.

❑ I feel pressure to be confident in my beliefs even when I have questions.

The articles, books, and conference speeches about the topic should tell you that you are not alone in feeling pressure. And you may argue that you thrive on pressure, that you are motivated by the deadlines. But here's what I know from watching others' lives and my own life: unrelenting pressure can turn into stress. And stress relief, done poorly, can wreck relationships, ministries, and lives. Regardless of our response to pressure, none of us are immune to its consistent presence. It shows up at our limits and edges, the boundaries where we interact with others, define ourselves and our work, and where we defend values and philosophies.

PRESSURE AT OUR EDGES

Pressure occurs when a force encounters resistance. And that happens at an edge. The line between the eighty-ton press and the watermelon are two surfaces, or edges, pressing against each other. The pressure of the press is greater than the pressure inside the watermelon, and the result is sloppy fruit salad. All of those pressures in the list come between our circumstances and our soul, between our expectations and our God-given competencies and calling, between ourselves and those around us, between our leadership and the people we are leading. We meet the world and minister to the world at the edges of our lives. There we define our lives, our boundaries, and how we protect what's important to us.

Pressure can push us to respond in ways we normally wouldn't; when the demands stack up on us they can short-circuit healthy and strategic responses, thoughts, and actions. Pressure and stress create fear and anxiety regarding our boundaries, and self-productive or defensive responses squeeze out time for reflection, creativity, and spiritually healthy practices. We often say that the pressures "put us on edge."

One of the tools I use with young leaders is the popular DISC profile (terrylinhart.com/disc). The tool gives me three results: (1) the "mask" the person shows to the world, (2) how the person will likely respond under pressure, and (3) the real self behind their exterior. Rarely are all three consistent. When working with others I am most interested in viewing the second result. I want to know how they think, respond, and lead when the pressure increases and the going gets tough.

NOT IN DESPAIR

Pressure is not new to God's people. Paul writes about it clearly in 2 Corinthians, a vulnerable letter he wrote to people he loved and was frustrated with. Paul says that when we accept a life of ministering God's reconciliation, we are also accepting a life full of pressure. We are afflicted, Paul says, or more accurately, we feel pressure (2 Cor 4:8). But we are not "crushed," according to familiar translations. But perhaps it would be clearer to say, *We are not squeezed into a corner with no way out*. It's one thing to feel pressure, it's another to be in despair at its presence and power.

We don't merely feel outside pressure; sometimes it bubbles up from within. As Paul looked back on his ministry, he noted that he often felt perplexed but was never in despair (v. 8). This could be translated "I feel lost, but not like I've lost out." Sometimes ministry presents situations where we don't know what to do, and we're in the dark as to what's ahead. Paul acknowledges this same feeling in his ministry, and we can take heart by his example, not being deterred in our faithfulness at our ambassadorial post. We have a role to play in our communities, a responsibility; and though it can be difficult, we are to persevere until the one who put us here moves us to our next post.

Paul ups the ante for those who say they are "all in" to a life in ministry. Though Paul was persecuted, he was never abandoned or left for ruin; though he was overtaken at times, he was never destroyed (2 Cor 4:9). Paul endured significant physical torture for his faith (2 Cor 11:24-26), and yet he recounts that he felt sustained and that the life of Jesus still could be seen in him (2 Cor 4:10). Though death was a constant possibility, Paul's faith and love (2 Cor 5:14) compelled him in the face of ministry pressures as he focused on the example of Christ (2 Cor 4:14).

Sometimes I find that my ministry focus has swiveled from the edges of my work to the center. Instead of spending my time and energy for the sake of the gospel and others, I have become too interested in seeking comfort and an easy schedule each week. And then Paul says, "All of this [suffering] is for your benefit, so that the grace that is reaching more and more people may cause thanksgiving to overflow to the glory of God" (2 Cor 4:15).

Paul endured seasons of pressure by focusing on Jesus and his supremacy in Paul's life. In moments of reflection on his life and ministry, he returned to the goal of knowing Christ more deeply, growing in Christlikeness, and engaging in mission with Christ (Phil 3:4-14). His confidence was in Jesus to work in and through him even in the midst of pressure, suffering, and opposition. Again, the process of developing self-awareness is not so we have more confidence in ourselves but so we can be more faithful and effective in the work that Christ has called us to do.

PRESSURE BECAUSE OF MY PERSONALITY

Mark had prepared for ministry his whole life: undergraduate studies, internship, volunteering, and four years on the job as an associate pastor. He loved the details, the numbers, the accounting. But he gradually became aware that effective ministry in his setting demanded more relational skills than he was able to give. His family, which was growing, was seeing less of him, and his work was draining. Finally, he realized that he was not designed for full-time ministry. He gave his notice, finished his responsibilities well, and began looking for work built around details. And he planned to keep working with small groups of students as a volunteer.

Some would look at Mark and say that he had failed or that being in ministry was a mistake. But he is a perfect example of a person who worked well, yet eventually recognized a gap between what the work called for and how he was built. It was a gap he couldn't recognize until he experienced the daily pressure at the boundary between life and who he is.

None of us look the same or are gifted the same, nor do we have the same capacities. In the body of Christ we each have different roles, functions, and approaches to what we are to be doing for God's kingdom (Rom 12:5; 1 Cor 12). Paul knew that people in the church often wish they had other roles or functions, and that people may not even know what their role should be: "God has placed the parts in the body, every one of them, just as he wanted them to be. If they were all one part, where would the body be? As it is, there are many parts, but one body" (1 Cor 12:18-20).

There's a reality-check moment in life when we realize that no matter how much we try, our personality, strengths, and weaknesses probably aren't going to change in significant ways. Like Mark, if we want to respond appropriately to our pressures, we need to understand our tendencies, preferences, and motivations, for it is in the search for awareness that we can learn about our strengths and weaknesses, our capacities and our fractures.[1]

Certain types of work get your attention and energy easier than others. You may like to lead upfront, organize, manage, create, or help; when you're doing your thing, you're "in the zone." Some of us love to create new stuff and will do so at the expense of managing things like, well, expenses. Like it or not, few of us get to operate in that sweet spot all week long—financial reports are a necessary part of our work.

Ministry requires tasks outside of our preferences. At these points young leaders often struggle, and pressures expose patterns that we may not have noticed before. Under pressure, whether intense moments or a daily grind, all my protective façades start to fall, and my character (honesty, denial, faithfulness, abandonment) and coping mechanisms (procrastination, self-medication, prayer) are revealed.

There are consistent actions you can take to help strengthen your ministry work when you are faced with a high-pressure situation.

1. Own your strengths and weaknesses. There are things you do very well, and others you don't enjoy or do well but you must do for your work. There's a reason that most interview committees ask about strengths and weaknesses, and there's a reason most novices can't answer the question well. Learning to acknowledge these rather than hide them will assist in your effectiveness as Christ's ambassador.

2. Develop resilience. When we think of an ambassador, we usually think of grace and consistency, a smooth exterior in the face of turmoil, an awareness that they represent a nation. The resilient capacity to bounce back, to be flexible, to respond more than react is developed over time. Though it may not seem like it, you're more resilient than you once were. Identify two or three things you can now handle with ease that ten years ago would have crushed you. Remember how those used to short-circuit your emotions and life? Now, think about two or three current things in your life that overwhelm you. In what ways can you begin to develop your capacity and resilience regarding them? In what ways can you be full of grace and consistency despite being pressed, perplexed, and knocked down?

3. Build your strengths, but challenge your weaknesses. Obviously, you possess natural and spiritual gifts that need to be used and strengthened. Those God-given talents should not be buried, but neither can you excuse nor hide behind your weaknesses. Writing is not my natural talent, but my ministry positions require it of me. I overcome this weakness by harnessing my love of being creative and by learning from others. And though I would be too quick to say writing isn't a strength, it's an area where I've seen God's strength and direction.

4. Remember who you follow. If we're not careful, self-focus leads to less about Jesus and God's power and provisions, and more about the clay of our lives. When we worry (usually because we desire control), we experience anxious pressure. Our task is to draw closer to Jesus, to nurture our trust in him, and to see our situations as he does. In the middle of intense pressure, God is often able to do great things for his glory.

PRESSURE WITH OTHER PEOPLE

Leadership is always defined in relationship to others, but leaders too rarely see the others as integral to their own assessment. If no one is following, we really aren't leading. And sometimes along the way we leaders forget that. Leading others creates consistent pressure, though, and the social arena of leadership is an area of inexperience for young leaders. We can't act like what is said is sufficient and words matter more than relationship. Though that may have once been the case in Western culture, it seems an increasingly dangerous strategy to enact. The new leadership dynamic is much more conscious of fit and team dynamics that require greater interdependence. I tell leaders, how you speak and when you speak communicate as much as what you speak.

BE AWARE: WHAT IS SOCIAL INTELLIGENCE?

Leaders who possess social intelligence exhibit one or more of these traits:

1. *Awareness.* Patty can recognize the social context of a group she's in. She understands how the power structure works, what's appropriate to the group's dynamics, and the role of the group within the larger community.

2. *Empathy.* After a few moments with someone, Derrick is able to understand the other person's emotional state. He can pick up on nonverbal cues, track what others are feeling or experiencing, and react appropriately.

3. *Social negotiation.* Kip has the ability to carry on a conversation with others without struggle. He can create smooth and effective interactions with others that benefit all involved in the conversation.

Leaders with social intelligence develop relationships because they demonstrate a sense of caring, responsiveness, and a genuine desire to understand before being understood. The quickest way to gauge this is by their listening abilities. Do they talk more than they listen?

Leaders who don't have well-developed social intelligence may seem slightly out of touch when it comes to communication and relationships. They are often characterized as cold, aloof, arrogant, or even abrasive. Too often these leaders are oblivious to how others react or feel about them. They do things that are off-putting and don't even know it.

I learned this while at a conference walking around the exhibit hall with my friend Reggie from Alabama. We walked past an exhibit, and the person there saw my name tag and mentioned that they liked a book I had written. I was then a new author and unsure how to respond. Thinking I was being humble, I mumbled my gratitude, smiled, and uncomfortably tried to move along.

"Wait!" Reggie said with Southern charm. "Are you going to receive the compliment?" I must have looked stunned by either the boldness or the idea that one had to receive a compliment. So, I stopped and turned back to say thank you and show appreciation for the kind words. Reggie, a careful listener and conversationalist, exemplified social intelligence in conversation.

This is an area that I've had to develop over the years. I am embarrassed to admit this, but my wife, Kelly, had to teach me words I never used growing up, like "congratulations" and "Oh, I'm so very sorry to hear about that." I've learned that "And what about you?" is a great conversation tool to make sure I'm focused on listening to others. Grace is at work here, isn't it? It's a social ability that resonates with God's unmerited favor toward us. No matter what is happening, we can find and express ourselves in ways that imitate God's love, patience, and generous nature to us and others.

A colleague of mine was teaching a course in spiritual formation. He started the first class with the usual overview material and watched the graduate students diligently taking notes. He had the class break into smaller groups to answer the question, How do you want to be known in five years? It's a question that draws out insights about the heart of a person. Then each person in the class introduced another student with what they had learned about that person. There were thoughtful and affirming introductions, revealing why people were pursuing spiritual growth and ministry. My friend watched to see that only one student was taking notes about who the other people were in the class. He reminded the class that ministry with others is less about knowing what's on the test and more about knowing the people we are traveling with.

Successful leaders are often described as those who *really* listen, have respect for others, demonstrate concern and compassion, and strive for understanding others' perspectives. They don't take a nonchalant approach to their work. They know that, due to the pull of the world and the flesh, we don't naturally drift toward better behavior without intentional spiritual formation. That drift is especially true in our social interactions.

So for a week try these actions drawn from what we know of successful leaders.

1. *Practice remembering.* At a gathering of friends listen for all the information about the struggles and victories people are in the middle of. Make written or mental notes. And then a week later, ask a person who won't be creeped out how the situation is going.

2. *Practice listening.* For ten minutes pay particular attention during a conversation with a friend. Thirty minutes later, off by yourself, repeat out loud as much of the exchange as you can remember. Try the exercise over several conversations until you are comfortable enough to repeat it to the friend.

3. *Practice perspective.* Before a meeting with a colleague, review everything you know about the current life situation of the person. Are they facing any struggles with family members? What personal successes have they had in the last month? What time of day is most productive for them? And how does this meeting fit with that productivity? Your goal in this exercise is learning to spend time giving yourself a better understanding of their situation.

HOW WE RESPOND TO PRESSURES

It is worth our best effort to not settle for second best, to let the pressures of ministry win the day, or to lose focus on what God is

SELF-CHECK

Productivity pressure tests leaders in four skills: vision, communication, systems, and money. Learn these and you'll help your organization and yourself.

1. *Managing vision.* Good vision is the ability to see ahead and behind while being fully aware of what matters in the present. What are your strengths and challenges as you fashion and share that vision? Would those you lead agree with you? What is their response to the substance of the vision?

2. *Managing communication.* Sharing the vision frequently is essential in organizational communication. But there is so much noise these days, and unless we're skillful, we create more noise. How do you ensure that your messages in print, social media, and face-to-face have a unified voice? What do your people say to each other about your communication practices?

3. *Managing systems.* Effective ministry requires administration, financial oversight, and clerical tasks. Systems can reduce risk, simplify decision making, and keep things running well during chaotic times. Further, systems that help you manage your own time and attention are essential. Do you have procedures, checklists, and policies for your team and yourself?

4. *Managing money.* Money isn't the most important concern in ministry, but any effective senior leader knows that many conflicts happen around money. When planning events, how can you accommodate the people who have little money as well as those who have plenty? What ways do you measure the return on the money people give to your ministries? How do you use those measures in your daily expenditures of ministry money?

calling you to do. The most important ministry work you have is the one right in front of you, wherever you are. You are not on your way to another event. There is no need to wish you had more people to follow your leadership. God has given you this moment, these people, this ministry to work with and invest in for his purposes. He is capable of moving you on or out when it's time.

For now, we are called to respond to pressures with wisdom and a resolve like that of the apostle Paul. "I press on to take hold of that for which Christ Jesus took hold of me," Paul said to his friends in Philippi. "Brothers and sisters, I do not consider myself yet to have taken hold of it. But one thing I do: Forgetting what is behind and straining toward what is ahead, I press on toward the goal to win the prize for which God has called me heavenward in Christ Jesus" (Phil 3:12-14).

FOR GREATER AWARENESS

1. On a scale of 1 to 10, with 10 being the highest, how high is your stress level most weeks? Right now? What causes the stress in your life most of the time (list as many causes as you can think of)?

2. If people could see your hidden life, what pressures that you feel would they likely be surprised to find?

3. What Scripture passages have helped you when you've experienced stress? Why do those particular verses help you?

4. Which of the three pressure areas—personal, social, and the pressure to produce—is most prominent for you?

5. List all the ways you respond when under pressure. Ask another person to describe you when you're under pressure. List those answers too. Now, look over your two lists and identify any items that aren't healthy. Reflect on why you respond that way.

7

THE FIRST INTENSE CONFLICT in a ministry setting is often a shock for people new to ministry. It's difficult to watch Christians equally committed to Christ disagreeing sharply. Young leaders are regularly unprepared for the first blitz of criticism they may get for changing something simple. The day-to-day functions of team ministry seem messier and less glamorous than advertised. And with teams of any size, not everyone will be pleased or happy with all decisions or directions.

Most leaders enter ministry with very few skills in conflict management. Schooling doesn't develop those skills, and most organizations don't have it as part of a training program. Conflict is a struggle between people holding beliefs, values, opinions, or perspectives that differ. The struggle can involve two people exchanging words in a meeting or can involve many countries and their armies. The struggle can emerge based on *how* we communicate due to our cultural background, ethnic context, temperament, and personality. The beliefs, values, and opinions socially formed by our life experiences, by good and bad organizational experiences, and by our education (formal and informal) shape our interactions with others in significant ways. It's no wonder that we need grace and to be gracious!

There are three realities you need to know. First, conflict in ministry is inevitable, and rarely enjoyable, because humans are involved. Second, conflict is healthy for a community that is on a mission to clarify the vision. Finally, it's not *that* conflict happens but *how* we do conflict that matters.

When James talks about conflict, he puts the blame on our pursuit of pleasures (Jas 4:1). But not all conflicts are selfish. We can have differences over two right things (Should the gospel go to Jews or also to Gentiles?), right and wrong (Should we cheat on our taxes or not?), two wrong things (Should we embezzle from this fund or that fund?), or even things that have no right or wrong answer (Is the blue carpet better than the green carpet?).

> If leaders can't learn how to navigate conflict, they will not last long in ministry.

Christian ministry leaders don't have a stellar track record of handling conflict. Some of us are assertive leaders—"it's my way or the highway" (because leaders lead, right?)—and we haven't developed the necessary graces. Some of us behave quite differently, acting nice every day and denying that anything is wrong. Most of us, though, operate somewhere in between. No matter our approach, conflict churns deeply and can easily grow into bitterness, resentment, and other emotional cesspools if not handled well. If leaders can't learn how to navigate conflict, they will not last long in ministry.

CONFLICT AND THE BIBLE

Wherever people work, live, and interact with others, there will be moments of conflict, and Scripture provides some clear examples of how best to handle it. Perhaps the most challenging description of the process is in the Sermon on the Mount (Mt 5–7). Jesus teaches us a relationship lifestyle rooted in resolved conflict.

1. The beginning of Matthew 5 describes the spirit with which we should approach each other in moments of tension, "Blessed are the merciful. . . . Blessed are the pure in heart. . . . Blessed are the peacemakers" (Mt 5:7-9).

2. Jesus says when his listeners are offering sacrifices at the altar and remember someone who has something against them, they are to leave the offering and be reconciled to the other person (Mt 5:23-24). The text is slightly ambiguous; Jesus doesn't say whether the other person is justified in their concern. So whether you are wrong, or they merely think you are wrong, restore the relationship.

3. Jesus says that his followers aren't to claim their right to retaliate in difficult situations. He identifies five possible situations and establishes this principle: look for ways to seek the good of the other person.

4. Jesus says that his followers are to love their enemies and pray for those who persecute them (Mt 5:44). This isn't a platitude. It's the way Jesus lived—and died. When hanging on the cross, Jesus prays, "Father, forgive them."

5. Jesus gives the disciples a prayer outline, which includes the phrase "forgive us our debts, as we also have forgiven our debtors" (Mt 6:12). Then, lest we miss the point, he picks that one phrase of the prayer to explain. If we forgive others, Jesus says, we will be forgiven. But if we do not, we won't be forgiven (Mt 6:14-15).

6. Then Jesus picks up on the idea of judging others (Mt 7:1-5), likening our offenses to logs and the offenses of others to twigs.

But he isn't minimizing the magnitude of offenses. People do awful things to others. He is saying that we have to resolve the things in our lives that blind us to truth, that break our relationship with God and others. Then we can work with others to address their offenses.

Sometimes we have disagreements that need to be addressed. As a tax collector Matthew knew a thing or two about conflict. He recorded Jesus' teaching on the steps to handling disputes (Mt 18:15-20). Person A is to go and show Person B their offense, just the two of them. If there is no resolution to the problem (either confession or realization that there wasn't an offense), then Person A is to bring in one or two other Christians as witnesses and to seek a resolution. If that fails, then the situation is to go before the church, whether the whole body or representative leadership. And if it can't be resolved there, then Jesus says one of the hard sayings we like to skip over, "Treat them as you would a pagan or a tax collector" (v. 17). That is, treat the person with compassion, but not as part of the community of believers.

The goal is to resolve it as quickly as possible by going directly and privately to the other person and seek resolution. Paul summarizes what Jesus says with a simple (and challenging) statement to the Roman church: "As far as it depends on you, live at peace with everyone" (Rom 12:18).

HANDLING CONFLICT WELL, ONCE AND FOR ALL

It's ironic that I'm writing a chapter on conflict because I am one who tries to avoid it as much as possible. Yet as a leader I have to navigate it regularly, even initiate it when confronting wrongs, and as a consultant I sometimes mediate conflict in churches, nonprofits, and ministries. Most of the time the problem is that people have not learned how to do conflict well.

What if we could solve that once and for all in our lives? What would happen if whenever we had a disagreement or conflict, there was no bitter residue for days and weeks afterwards? What if forgiveness was as much our recognized character as our entrepreneurial drive and talents? The following are ten principles that will help you navigate conflict well. I wish I had known these in the early days of my ministry. They would have helped me resolve many problems.

1. Work in slowly from the edges of the conflict. As I write this, Kelly is assembling a jigsaw puzzle nearby. She didn't start with the center, but first found the edge pieces and framed the puzzle. Then she worked inward. Too often, we want to run to the middle of a conflict when we haven't framed the whole picture.

There are a couple ways to lay out the frame. First, take the time to listen to the people involved in the conflict. As we read in Proverbs: "In a lawsuit the first to speak seems right, until someone comes forward and cross-examines" (Prov 18:17). We need to take time to identify and listen to all the voices.

Second, take the time to understand the scope of the conflict. We often hear, "Everyone is upset" when only two or three people are upset. We hear, "Everything is broken" when only one process is broken. It takes more time than we think to understand the situation. But if we rush to our solution, we might miss God's incredible blessings as he works out this conflict.

2. Understand how conflict erupts. To frame well we need to know what often causes group conflict to go wild. I've learned so much from Pastor Dave Engbrecht at Nappanee Missionary Church (Indiana) through the years. One of his consistent teaching points is "let's make sure we do conflict well." There's no absence of high-powered leaders on his church staff or in the congregation, and "doing conflict well" doesn't mean there aren't intense conversations or problems. But conflict has never resulted in divisiveness, and each year he gathers his leadership teams to remind them of what causes ministry teams to "go rogue."

WHAT CAUSES MINISTRY TEAMS TO GO ROGUE

- Selfishness: the inability to play team ball
- Pettiness: letting small things become big
- Personal agendas
- The inability to have frank and honest discussions
- Failure for leadership to watch themselves—individually and as subgroups
- Low level of commitment to the cause
- Lack of clarity of the mission

Think back to the last conflict that your group had. Which of these contributed to it? What was your responsibility to the conflict? What would have minimized the severity of the conflict?

(Adapted from Dave Engbrecht, pastor of Nappanee Missionary Church, www.nmconline.net.)

3. Discuss with many voices, leave with one voice. After addressing any intense conflict, when the meeting is over and the decision made, the group is to be of one voice.[1] There is to be no leak of who said what and when. Unity is a demonstration that the issue has been truly resolved. Mistrust that can develop due to a lack of discretion will limit the potential and effectiveness going forward. And this is the area where many organizations and churches fall short.

4. Never intentionally have conflict with other leaders in front of those you lead. Some may question whether it's bad to display leadership conflict in public, but discretion is a worthy goal to pursue.

When people watch their leaders having conflict, too often we lose significant credibility. Whenever a confrontation is necessary, take the strategy that Priscilla and Aquila used with Apollos—discuss and resolve it in private (Acts 18:26).

5. Never resolve conflict via email or social media. Conflict is rarely resolved until the people are face-to-face. I know some may disagree with this, but I feel so strongly about this that in all of my organizations I have a policy in place to not engage in conflict via email or social media. Here's why: at our best, we can misunderstand written communication. Even with emojis, we can't put into writing all the information and feeling that is conveyed through tone of voice, facial expressions, gestures, and pauses.

It's easy for someone to attack a leadership decision on Facebook. When this happens, refrain from the temptation to respond in kind. Instead, using Jesus' teaching to go the second mile, reach out to the person privately. When the topic is delicate or explosive, take the time to make yourself as present as possible to resolve conflict.

6. Though conflict should be resolved quickly, make sure to let the emotional fervor fade first. In Christian circles we like to quote "don't let the sun go down on your anger." This advice comes in a discussion in Ephesians 4 about how we are to relate to each other. But the text is not saying that we have to talk with everyone we are angry with before sunset each day. I've discovered that sleeping on matters for a night sometimes helps. I have a friend who gets so fired up (meaning that he gets passionate) that he tells people, "I'll get back to you within seventy-two hours" so he can calm down, think through the problem, and not respond from pure emotion in the moment.

7. Learn not to say whatever comes to your mind. I've seen this pattern too often, and people who speak without regard to relationship aren't usually treasured by colleagues. This is something people may wish they could tell us, but don't want to hurt our feelings. "Speaking the truth in love" doesn't give us license to say the first thing that comes to our minds.

One pastor I know is aware that he could easily get into debates. So he always takes a blank legal pad into meetings where people will be airing grievances, and he simply takes notes throughout the meeting. Writing disciplines him to pay attention to what is being said rather than anticipating his responses. If you talk more than the other people you're with, you will want to check to see if you're listening well enough and if your conversation is well-filtered.

> If you talk more than the other people you're with, you will want to check to see if you're listening well enough and if your conversation is well-filtered.

8. Set limits to strong statements. Though sometimes we have to initiate conflict, the bigger issue is that we need to know when we're doing so. We leaders can speak our mind so often that we aren't aware of the effect on those around us. The older we get, the more comfortable and unaware of this we can become.

I often talk about "coupons" as a way to be aware of forcefulness in groups.[2] I tell groups that when we step into a meeting or a group, we only have one coupon in our pocket. This coupon lets us make a strong and uncomfortable statement, comment, or point that may conflict with others' views. It's not an excuse for causing needless pain or for reminding everyone about our obsession. But it is permission to be direct. Usually, but not always, once we have used the coupon, we're done.

I was in a meeting with a leader who had heard me teach on the coupon principle. He was fired up about a topic but realized he already had made some strong statements in that meeting. He looked at me and said, "I'm playing my second coupon" and then he did, which was fine. The coupon principle had still served its purpose: it helps us manage the number of moments when we're being forceful or we're initiating conflict.

9. Resist defensiveness. Almost no one naturally likes criticism, even the constructive kind. But sometimes we feel attacked when someone appropriately identifies issues that need to be resolved.

A staff member was thinking through how she talks with her boss and realized that every time her boss identified something in the church that needed attention, she defended what she had done. If the toilet paper dispenser was empty, she explained how busy the church had been the day before. If a lock wasn't working, she explained how many times they had tried to fix it.

The boss wasn't being critical or accusatory, but was merely mentioning issues that needed to be resolved. An empty paper towel dispenser on a Sunday morning needs to be filled, not explained. But my friend interpreted it as an attack and immediately defended herself and the people who reported to her. Her defensiveness was keeping the conversation from turning to solutions.

Some things need to be defended. This doesn't mean that shepherds don't defend the sheep from attack. But defending our reputation in conversations with family, friends, and coworkers wastes the energy and attention that could go toward taking care of the issue. A proverb goes to the heart of the problem: "Pride only breeds quarrels," the sage says, "but wisdom is found in those who take advice" (Prov 13:10 NIV 1984).

Bob Goff is an attorney who defends victims in courtrooms in this country and in orphanages overseas. When his clients are called to give depositions to be interviewed about their story, he tells them to sit with the backs of their hands on their legs, and their palms open, facing up. By not clenching their fists, they will stay calm and not get defensive. And, as Goff says, "When people get angry or defensive they tend to make mistakes."[3] It's good counsel.

10. Be personally committed to excellent communication. I know that not all conflict comes from poor communication. We can have conflict even when we clearly understand each other. Nevertheless, I don't want my communication failures to cause conflict. For example, when there is poor communication, people dream up wild rumors that lead to conflict and chaos. I had a friend who was so inattentive to his communication that more conflict and mistrust developed in his organization than the others in his community.

When I am at my best, I do all that I can to eliminate confusion, to affirm the value of the people I work with, to listen and then to speak. I practice the things in this list. I know that I am not always at my best. But a godly leader should attempt nothing less.

WHERE CONFLICT IS PART
OF THE LANDSCAPE

To this point I've spoken of our own posture when it comes to conflict. We all have moments when we think others are causing conflict, then we see the real cause in the mirror. However, we can work in environments where the issues are not our own. The problems can run deep within the organizations or churches where we work. They are often present before we arrive and will remain after we leave. The following are three kinds of people who are chronic sources of conflict.

Controlling people. Research into church conflict shows that leaders are often fired due to conflict over who is in control. What usually sparks the problems is a change or an attempt to change. A new staff member attempts to introduce changes and discovers someone who feels they should have been consulted. A pastor arrives at a new church and discovers that someone won't issue them a key to the kitchen.

When you think there may be a pattern of control, try this process. See if there are a series of conflicts around the same person, discern whether control is at the heart of the problem, determine what steps you are willing to take, and release control into God's hands. In cases of controlling people, the surface issue will sound spiritual, thoughtful, or managerially intelligent. Making sure you can see the point of conflict will allow you to move carefully toward discerning the real issue.

Antagonistic personality. Truthfully, some folks struggle in leadership because their personalities are like sandpaper to others. They have difficulty keeping jobs and being close with peers. We may be asked to work alongside them. Rather than react to them, I've learned to draw them closer in. It seems counterintuitive and still doesn't fix the core problem, but the practice has allowed my relationship with these types of folks to be productive. The truth is that as I spend longer hours getting to know the real person behind the coarse exterior, I can work better with and advocate for them. And I find that as a trusting relationship develops, there are opportunities for honest discussions about developing warmth and empathy.

Detached leadership. It's difficult to know how to be successful when leaders don't provide clear direction and are inattentive to results. I have worked in such environments, so I'm familiar with the positives and negatives. There is a welcome freedom in these situations, but there is also a lack of motivation to work hard when it's unclear for why you should strive to do so. Expectations are often not met because there is a lack of distinct guidelines for what needs to happen. If the leader doesn't clearly lay out the direction toward success, others will simply not follow.

Learn to seek out the direction and affirmation you need rather than getting frustrated in waiting. Offer clear proposals and plans, which will provide a framework for action and a path for others. Look for purpose in the organization and in the work itself rather than in the leader. If you can't find impact for the kingdom of God, step aside. Because wasting resources on confusion is not stewardship.

The important aspect with these situations is to be aware of the difficult dynamics you are experiencing. Then you can prayerfully make sure that God wants you to be there. Just because these kinds of people are in our lives doesn't give us license to be disobedient to what God wants for us.

SILENT BUT DEADLY:
PASSIVE-AGGRESSIVENESS

The source of much conflict is readily apparent, but I want to spend time exploring conflict that is more insidious. We all know what active aggressiveness is. Fists up, voices raised, combative attitudes. We know less about passive-aggressiveness. And yet this hidden approach to conflict may be more present in our organizations—or our lives—than the active kind. Before I explain, I want to tell you something about how I grew up.

Some of us grew up in a culture where we didn't express anger much. It may be more accurate to say that we couldn't express anger. I remember long road trips in the family station wagon (seatbelts optional, of course, as we played in the back of the station wagon with the back window rolled down). If I ever became angry about something, I would get silent. That's right, I would withdraw. *I'll show them. I won't talk to them!* Now that I'm a parent, I know that I wasn't punishing my family in those moments; I was blessing them with silence!

I still struggle with honesty about conflict. Ask me how I'm doing and I'll say fine, even though I could be secretly steaming. My wife, Kelly, knows better, of course, and just smiles at me whenever I try that with her. But that's how I learned to handle things. I'm always fine, even when I'm not. Just ask me.

At its core, passive-aggressiveness is a disconnect between what we say and what we do. It is deception, a dishonesty that is antagonistic to others and to God's desires: "Enemies disguise themselves with their lips, but in their hearts they harbor deceit" (Prov 26:24). Organizations can hold meetings to discuss policy and procedures, everyone around the table can say they agree, but someone can sabotage progress by not meeting deadlines and generating indirect hostility. People can make caustic comments in conversations but then add "I was only joking" or "Why are you mad?" to avoid direct, honest dialogue.

Passive-aggressiveness can create another disconnect when there is an inability or unwillingness to communicate directly and honestly. Sometimes leaders have to delay decisions or releasing a communication. That's normal for any organization. However, it can sometimes morph into something more where we stretch the truth, don't tell the truth, and even cover for others in dishonest or even deceptive ways. Whether it's due to insecurity or overconfidence, I'm amazed how quickly we in Christian leadership can be tempted to deceive and lie to those we lead, but we give the practice other names. If we aren't attentive, that sinful deception will only grow and end up damaging many others' lives, ruining our message, and staining our legacy.

How easy is it for someone you lead to get the truth from you? How would those you lead answer that question? Would others say that there is a high level of trust in

> How easy is it for someone you lead to get the truth from you? How would those you lead answer that question? Would others say that there is a high level of trust in your group? Is there a group who might say there is not a high level of trust?

your group? Is there a group who might say there is not a high level of trust?

Passive-aggressiveness destroys trust, and trust is a precious commodity for leaders. Trust is the close companion to genuine love and true grace. When we're passive-aggressive, we deceive by presenting ourselves one way but working toward another outcome. We do so out of fear, when our autonomy or authority is threatened, or when our plan is opposed and we don't have much power or can't really say anything.

Psychologists say passive-aggressiveness shows up when the following are true.

1. Anger is socially unacceptable (that is, being a "good" Christian means not being angry).

2. Anger is expressed in alternative ways, since we are actually angry inside.

3. We rationalize our position as the victim or as the voice of reason.

4. We have a way to get back at someone who wrongs or opposes us.

5. We have a way to influence others' emotional responses and behavior.[4]

The classic passive-aggressive person in the Bible is the older brother of the prodigal son (Lk 15). Missionary counselor and former psychology professor Ronald Koteskey points out that the older son met six of the seven total criteria for passive-aggressiveness in three short verses! The older brother

- resisted carrying out routine social tasks: he refused to go to his brother's party (v. 28);

- complained of being unappreciated by others: his father never gave him a party (v. 29);

- was sullen and argumentative: he argued with his father (v. 29);

- criticized and scorned authority: he criticized his father's party for the squandering son (v. 30);

- expressed envy and resentment toward those more fortunate: he resented that the fattened calf was killed for his brother (v. 30);

- voiced exaggerated complaints of personal misfortune: he had "slaved" for years (v. 29)[5].

Take a couple minutes to think through your own behaviors and thoughts. Ask yourself these questions:

- When was the last time you didn't share an honest view about a topic, even when asked?

- Have you ever become upset with someone but didn't let them know why? Who was it? Why were you afraid to explain? How did you act toward them during the next week?

- Have you seen someone praise someone in public, but criticize that same person in private?[6]

Passive-aggressiveness is easier to spot in others than our own lives. There is likely an underlying cause for passive-aggressiveness. It can be due to a fear of failure (a desire for perfection), a fear of rejection (a desire to be liked), or a fear of conflict (a desire for harmony). It's crucial to understand the root of the issue so that it can be addressed head-on.

Suppressed aggression looks like sarcasm, failing to complete a task, procrastination, stubbornness, chronic lateness, and even grumpiness. I've seen some of the sweetest people in the world unable to express their disagreement, so they start to regularly show up late to work, "forget" to complete tasks, and work with intentional inefficiency. It's very common among volunteers who have no option to express displeasure with the vocational leaders they help.

It's important to add that indirect communication is different from passive-aggressiveness, and I've tried to be precise in this section. Some cultural contexts value indirect communication as a way to maintain harmony and avoid shame, even in the midst of conflict. I work and teach often in Southeast Asia and have many dear friends and colleagues there. I am sensitive to their cultural form of communication and navigating conflict there. We need to have that same sensitivity in our home communities as well, recognizing that some families, ethnic groups, and denominational traditions use indirect methods of conflict resolution.[7] And we have to adjust if we want to be effective peacemakers.

MOVING FORWARD

Regardless of our experience or ministry context, the inability to handle and navigate conflict and defensiveness can be blind spots for some Christian workers. The reality is that we cannot avoid conflict, but at the same time we need to be committed to doing conflict well.

What about you? Do you find yourself easily bothered by what others say or do? Do you lose sleep over the fact that others don't respond to you like you believe they should? Do you often say "I'm offended" or something similar? Do you find yourself in small arguments more often than you have been in the past? People new to leadership can be more confident than their experience level would support. Further, if we're honest, we can be quite selfish no matter our experience level. The humbling part in all of this is that often what irritates us about others is what we're working on ourselves. In fact, in my coaching of young leaders I often say, "Your irritations may look a lot like you." The principle is this: *the things about others that irritate us teach us something about ourselves.*

Wherever humans work and live with one another, there will be conflict. That includes the church, Christian ministries, and non-profit settings. Unfortunately, Christian ministries have been notorious for not handling conflict well. We need to lead the charge in our ministry settings to create the context and guidelines for handling conflict well. By doing so, we help foster a dynamic in our community that is warm, inviting, and effective. The health and unity of your group and its collective Christlike character will be a floodlight in your community announcing something rare in these divisive days.

FOR GREATER AWARENESS

I use this series of eight questions to help gain perspective on conflict, whether it involves me or not. Use this process as your next steps for this chapter.

After periods of prayer and spiritual reflection, I ask:

1. In one sentence, what is the problem?

2. Who is involved (names, roles, relationships)?

3. What are people saying that is wrong?

4. Is there a history, underlying issue, or context for the problem, and how long has it existed?

5. Was there a trigger event? Has it expanded since then?

6. In one word, what is the category of this conflict (vision, sin, preferences, feelings, relationship, or something else)?

7. According to the people involved, what would resolve the conflict?

8. If you had a godly outside mediator, what would that person say is the problem, and what would be the recommended resolution?

To discern more about your own passive aggressiveness, reflect on these questions.

1. Do I resent anyone's authority in my life?

2. Where am I resisting the direction of the ministry I serve?

3. As a leader, am I facilitating passive resistance by leading a culture of poor communication and by suppressing open dialogue?

4. How would others describe my level of generosity to others and my openness to their ideas and input?

5. Have I recently denied my feelings or ideas to others when I knew that it wasn't how I truly felt? Explain.

8

THE PAPER USED FOR STANDARD letter writing and school essays is 8.5 x 11 inches, or 93.5 square inches. Most teachers require one-inch margins for class papers. That's the standard we've become accustomed to seeing. But have you ever stopped to consider what percentage of the page that margin occupies? When I ask people, most answer anywhere from 15 to 25 percent.

But a one-inch margin on a standard sized paper is 37.4 percent of a page's area. More than one-third of the page is given to space. And that's just around the edges. When you double-space the lines of text, a majority of the paper is blank.

The empty border helps us focus on the printed text. It creates a comfortable feel for our eyes. Stylish magazines help readers focus on the text and images by using large amounts of margin on each page. Sometimes we use even more margin in catalogs and on blogs.

Sometimes people think that margin (sometimes called "white space") is wasteful and inefficient. They pack as much print as possible on the page.

Single-spaced text, half-inch margins. It may be efficient, but it is achingly ineffective. Have you ever seen a page packed with text from top to bottom and side to side? I get tired looking at it, even before I begin reading it.

Obviously, I'm inviting you to think about something other than publishing. I want you to think about your life. Margins and space in our lives, blank spaces on our calendars, can give us room to think, to form thoughts, to group ideas, and to refresh our soul and thinking. We know that, but few of us live like we do. We hustle to be productive, packing our lives with interaction and activity. As soon as we wake, we scroll through our smartphone apps. Right before bed we're checking as well. Research has shown both practices to be harmful to us, but we keep doing it. In between we are constantly active, striving toward *something*. We long for more time for healthy living and regret how little time we have for it.

Margins are curious things once you become aware of how large they are. It looks like 37 percent (at least!) of a normal page is, uh, *empty*. Well, we think it is empty, but it's not. It is full of *margin*. Think about it. Margin plays a very important role. Margin has substance, and it intersects with how we live (our heart), how we think (our mind), and how we act (our hands).We create new thoughts, we respond, and we reflect by writing in the margins. Our thumbs hold the page secure at the margins. We focus because there are margins.

What if we took the margin principle and applied it to our lives? Think of the roughly 112 waking hours we have every week. What if 37 percent of our week were unstructured and available for establishing healthy practices in our lives? What would you do if you had six hours a day available as margin? It's creative white space, 37 percent of your day, to be used for being healthy in heart, soul, mind, and strength. What would you do?

Let's think about how we spend those hours now. Watching a movie? On the smartphone? Working around the house? Out for a night on the town? Reading? Praying? Exercising? Spending time with family? There is debate on what constitutes good recreation and healthy practices, so I'll leave it up to you, but here's my advice—healthy margins are worth your best.

You can see the challenge. We fill those hours with activities that may not be healthy. Our days off don't always look much different from our work days. Keeping a sabbath focused on how good and trustworthy God is seems a rare practice even for those in Christian ministry. It's no wonder that we soon find ourselves running on empty, with little margin for anything to go wrong. What if our lives were marked with a maturity rooted in rich times of study, reflection, and prayer? How would these disciplines affect the work we care about?

Imagine the gymnast on the balance beam. She performs her routine on a long beam just four inches wide. A trained gymnast knows that four inches is enough, although there is little margin for error to the right or left as she flips and cartwheels back and forth. But it feels as if people in ministry run their lives like they're balancing on a two-inch-wide beam, half the space that we need. We've tried to run without margin for so long that we get stretched too thin, all the way to the edge. So, when a wind comes that blows against us or shakes our standing, we easily fall. Consider these examples:

- We procrastinate to the very edge of time, then something goes wrong. We are creating our own stress, and we panic under the pressure.

- We wait to prepare for a talk and give a half-hearted lesson, thinking that is our best effort. We're becoming used to less than our best.

- We fail to stay current on ministry-related conversations, not growing in skills and understanding.

- We give little time to studying and find ourselves unable to answer people's hard questions.

- We falter and are embarrassed when we are asked questions that should be easily answered. We know deep down that our lack of study makes us feel this way.

When I come alongside and coach people in leadership, I look for the margins of how they're doing spiritually, emotionally, mentally, socially, and physiologically. I look for how narrow their balance beam is and how quickly life can knock them off balance. Then, I look for a third kind of margin, which I'll share later in this chapter.

MARGIN IN GOD'S DIRECTION

When we look at the margin God built into the lives of his people, we usually think of sabbath. We know that the Ten Commandments include sabbath. God's people were called to devote one day a week to not working. But God was interested in more than just a once-a-week time of rest. In his conversational commentary on Nehemiah, Jon Swanson identifies six margin-giving routines in the life of Israel.[1]

Daily routines. In the beginning of his story Nehemiah prays morning and evening about the broken walls of Jerusalem. This seems to be part of his normal practice, not just because of the crisis. In this, he echoes the practice of the Levites, who prayed in front of the altar morning and evening. Stopping to pray acknowledges the presence of God in our ministry day.

Weekly routines. Sabbath was a weekly reminder of God's rest after creation and God's rescue of his people from Egypt. We can pause daily, but we need a longer time each week to refresh and remember. To set aside our lists and remember that the strength and direction come from God. For workers in ministry this may need to be a day other than Sunday.

Monthly reminders. Leadership research says leaders should reinforce vision every twenty-eight days or so. That need, which is built into our hearts, may be why God told the people to make a sacrifice every new moon. We need time to stop and recalibrate our hearts.

Annual routines. Passover, the Feast of Tabernacles, and the Feast of Weeks are examples of annual celebrations in the life of Israel. God didn't intend these to be legalistic restrictions. He meant them to be times when the people would tell the stories of God's work to their children. They were times for eating together and sharing food with those who were lacking.

Reminders every seven years. God had laid out a sabbath year, a time when debts were cancelled and the land wasn't worked. The people were supposed to remember that God had given them the Promised Land—created by God, given by God, watered by God. But the people didn't practice this routine, and the exile was a way to give the land, and the people, the margin they hadn't given themselves.

Once-in-a-lifetime celebrations. The dedication of the wall that Nehemiah and the people built was a unique time of celebration. But the biggest celebration Israel was to observe was the year of Jubilee, every fifty years. It was a sabbath of sabbath years. It was supposed to be huge. And there is no record that Israel ever kept it.

Stopping long enough to pray morning and evening brackets the ministry day. A weekly sabbath resets our lives around God's time, God's people, and God's presence. A monthly celebration recalibrates our vision. Annual holidays renew the stories of God that we are part of. Regular, but infrequent, long breaks give us restoration. And once-in-a-lifetime events tell us what we are living toward.

It occurs to me that if we add up the sabbaths, the monthly celebrations and the feasts, God laid out a life in which about a third of the year was margin. I know that Paul talks to the Colossians about not judging others for how they keep the New Moon festival (Col 2:16). But God was laying out margins to be filled by him. When we fill them with obligation, we are adding more work, not margin. But if we fill them with worship, play, community, rest, and relationship, we may find the context for spiritual growth that God intended.

MARGINS FOR THE HEART

We are to love God with our soul, strength, mind, and heart (Deut 6:5). With the heart we revere Christ as Lord and are strengthened (1 Pet 3:15; 1 Thess 3:13). Our heart makes us do some unexpected things. We'll drive for hours at odd times of the day just to see a girlfriend or boyfriend. We'll dress in ways unfit for the dinner table when attending sporting events. We do crazy things for our affections. I have a scar on my right thumb from celebrating a well-timed Willie McGee triple in the 1982 World Series. (My hand sliced through a ceiling light when I jumped up from the couch in joy.)

Which margin crumbles first? It isn't how we act or think, but our affections. I've rarely met a Christian worker who says they're satisfied with their devotional life. And as you know, the word *devotion* is about affections. When we are devoted to someone or something, our hearts are in it, our passion is engaged. And every moment with the one we are devoted to helps that passion deepen.

We are invited to be spiritually formed in our lives, exhibiting Christlikeness to the world through the power of the Holy Spirit. This requires a different approach from one shaped by consumerism, where the focus is on what we can get out of it and how our spiritual life serves us. We serve Jesus Christ in ministry, and he calls us to follow him. He exhibited a life of prayer and time away. So should we.

Earlier, I discussed the ups and downs of our emotions while in ministry. It's worth our time to reflect on margins of our emotions. This is easy to write about but hard to practice. Those who are new to ministry need to think about how they will maintain resiliency, renew their emotions, and grow in emotional maturity. This area is a common tripping point for Christian workers. As mentioned earlier, ministry is like an eighty-ton press that continues to push down on us, splintering our balsa veneer and crumbling defenses while oozing out our hidden emotional substance. Then we see spikes in our emotional responses; we react too quickly and have no room for wisdom and reflection. The press of ministry knocks some of us off balance, and we either need a healthy dose of forgiveness and grace, or we quit.

Is managing your emotions like walking on a balance beam? Do you find that you can be off the beam in a hurry? If you want to create margin for your heart, I'd like to suggest three practices.

Fifteen minutes of morning coffee or tea with God. Bill Hybels describes a morning practice of spending fifteen minutes in a chair with a Bible, a journal (if you wish), and God. I have a friend who has been doing this for a couple of years. The chair was his grandfather's. He gets up at 5:30, makes coffee, and then sits down at 5:45 to read and write and pray. The first words in his journal are often, "Good morning, Father." The Scripture reading can be from a sermon, from Proverbs, or prompted by a question that he is wrestling with. And the prayer, which usually happens in the journal, is informal and conversational. Often, he'll write the question, and the answer will come to him. Though it sounds a little odd to say that, he writes, "I know that the writing slows my mind to prayer speed. And interacting with the Bible feels like conversation."[2]

Restore your soul with things that give you life. The psalmist says of the shepherd, "He leads me beside quiet waters, he refreshes my soul" (Ps 23:2-3). So what work of God gives you life? One way to tell if something moves you at the soul level is if the experience makes you weep. One friend loves live, unamplified music. The sound of a children's choir or an orchestra can captivate him. Another pastor friend loves to attend worship at a church of another denomination. Participating in a service without having any responsibilities to lead gives a freedom. Take a few minutes and reflect on the kinds of experiences that restore your soul. Wilderness. Art. Crafting wood. Flying. Jamming with friends.

If you can identify experiences like these, schedule them.

Walk if you can, with someone if possible. Not everyone can walk. But if you can walk or ride or roll, build that kind of activity into your schedule. I understand that it seems strange to include physical activity in practices of the heart. But walking can help your emotional health as well as your actual heart. It is slow enough to allow you to think, but active enough to get you away from technology, sitting, and the usual distractions of your day. Walking with someone can build community. Exercise helps with thinking. And think about the number of conversations Jesus had with people along the road.

MENTAL MARGINS

"The one who gets wisdom loves life; the one who cherishes understanding will soon prosper" (Prov 19:8). As the wise writer of Proverbs teaches, the older you get, the more you realize how important knowledge is. The way we write wisdom into the white space of our minds gives us resources for offering and receiving counsel, for choosing between alternatives, for setting value on the outcomes of our potential choices. There are many ways to gain wisdom. We're shaped by who we spend time with and what we read. We've talked in other places about relationships, so here I want to talk about reading.

We shape our thinking in dramatic ways through disciplined reading. I'm surprised by how strongly various experts challenge today's leaders about reading. Bill Hybels wrote, "I have little patience with leaders who get themselves into leadership binds and then confess that they haven't read a leadership book in years."[3] John Wesley reportedly told young leaders to read or get out of the ministry.

If we looked back over the last month at what we watched and read, in what subject would others say we're developing our expertise? In our Google age, knowing stuff seems outdated when you can just Google it. That quick-access culture works against practices (like study) that work to cultivate depth of thought. Unless we're intentional, the Internet will shift our focus toward pop culture instead of wisdom and knowledge sources.

These influences affect more than just our knowledge building, though. Few face-to-face conversations take place without frequent checks of a smartphone to see who else wants our attention. Binge watching a video series over a weekend is more appealing than a two-hour retreat for prayer and Scripture study. Leaders today have to give consistent attention to how they are growing mentally in an age of

> "To the person, the best leaders I know are prolific readers. The most successful people I know consume written content at a pace that far exceeds that of the average person. If you want to improve your station in life, as well as the lives around you—read more. . . . I have little patience for those leaders who are 'too busy' or 'too smart' or 'too important' to learn. Put simply, if you're not learning, you have no business leading."
>
> Mike Myatt, *Hacking Leadership* (Hoboken, NJ: Wiley, 2013), 124

hyperreality and soundbite thinking. Critical thinking and mature wisdom are the skills that separate leaders, influencers, and decision makers from others. Those attributes contribute to leadership success and, ironically, higher pay in the corporate world. And the devaluation of education and knowledge can slip into how we think about church and ministry leadership.

Developing our depth of thinking and wisdom will help us address our tendency to make impulsive decisions. Christian ministries can be notorious for swinging on a pendulum toward the latest trends. We grab at what works without much consideration of anything more. And ten years later we grab at something different. So we see ministries running to and fro as they try to navigate the cultural currents.

Margins help us develop our innovative leadership thinking. There's a reason we seem more creative when we're younger: we have the time to be! There's a common rule that we're most creative when we're working at about 60 percent of capacity. When was the last time that your work only took up 60 percent of your waking hours? Some of us fill these hours to their capacity, wearing ourselves out in the process and losing our creative space.

When we establish margins for mental development, we are careful with what we put on our schedules, and we allow for some play space to reflect, create, and not be taking in new information. What fuels your innovative thinking? When was the last time you had a genuinely creative idea? What will it take for you to stay innovative, fresh, and relevant to the times as you age? What can you instill in your life now that will foster your creativity?

Here are two questions to help you think about creating margin in your mind.

What was the last book you read? Mike is a leader in a mission agency. He never was a reader, until someone challenged his team to read ten books in a year. He started reading. Then he started asking other leaders for recommendations. Whether a book was short or long did not matter. He just kept reading. Now, he's known as the guy who always has a recommendation for a book to read. And he annoys his pastor by asking, "What's the last book you read?" So that's my question for you. If you can't answer it, consider being like Mike.

As you develop your reading habit, it's important to read widely. For instance, are some of the authors you are reading different from you? Do you read books authored by both men and women? Are you being stretched by a variety of people from different perspectives and backgrounds? Or are all the people you are reading of the same generation, racial/ethnic background, and denominational tradition?

What question about God are you answering? What characteristic of God are you tracing through Scripture? This question is inspired by Pam Slim, who talks about creating a "body of work." She defines this as "everything you create, contribute, affect, and impact. . . . It is the personal legacy you leave at the end of your life, including all the tangible and intangible things you have created."[4]

A body of work is easy to see when we think about writers. We know that after forty years studying Paul, N. T. Wright produces commentaries and theology books. John Maxwell writes on leadership and has sold more than 20 million books. He started his studies of leadership and service when he was still in high school and his dad gave him a reading list.

But your body of work doesn't have to be books. It can be conversations with young leaders, or well-crafted worship events, or thoughtful, quiet, hospital visits that put flesh on your understanding of God's compassion or glory or relationships. If you started pursuing answers to a question about God or about ministry, imagine what you would know and live.

MARGINS FOR OUR WORK

At some point we have to recognize that life can't be lived well with others when we're pressed past the margins of our time. If by day three of a vacation we are ready to get back to work, we may be striving for something counter to the biblical view of life lived well. I'm as driven as most, and I love to work, but I'm a better person when in my margins I'm taking the time to read, having meaningful conversation with others, enjoying nature, and giving my time and attention to others.

As a teenager I wanted to be in the Navy, and I learned about a tactic that attack submarines employ when searching for enemy vessels. Submarines conduct a series of sprints interspersed with periods of drifting. When drifting, they float at three knots and are actually quieter than the surrounding ocean due to their sound-absorbent anechoic coating. When a vessel is heard some distance away, the sub will go very deep and sprint at 20 knots or more to get closer and ahead of the target. The subs do not sprint for long periods because they cannot listen well while moving fast. After a sprint, they drift again, listening for their objective.

I've found the sprint-drift principle helpful for Christian ministry and leadership. There are times when we need to sprint, moving quickly and efficiently. It can last for weeks, perhaps months, but it needs to be followed by quieter times of drifting and listening. Each fall I sprint for four months with a full schedule of conferences, teaching, and speaking engagements. After that, I have a period of drifting before returning to a shorter sprint period in spring, when I have room to work on writing projects. That is followed by a short drift period in May before the summer season of consulting. I bet your year has its own sprint-drift seasons as well. The key is not to sprint so long that no amount of drifting will bring you back to normal speed. We should never let the fast speeds be an excuse for abandoning the necessary spiritual disciplines or to push aside intimacy with Jesus.

How does this look in ministry? Church worship leaders know that there are incredible expectations and opportunities around Christmas. We plan services and specials. We pray for clarity in every element of the services for people who only attend around Christmas. We rehearse many extra people. And we survive. But what do we do the Sunday after Christmas? Some people start working on Easter services. Those who understand the principle of sprint and drift know that a little space in January will actually help with Easter by allowing the congregation and the worship leader to recover from an intense Advent season.

Sprint-drift has been part of my life for a long time. I learned it when I was a serious runner. There is a method of training designed to build a runner's speed and capacity. Fartlek training requires running fast for a short distance and then jogging until you recover and your heart rate and breathing slow. Then you sprint again. It looks odd and feels strange to do, but the exertion during the sprints helps develop endurance and grow the capacity for more. The potential for success in future races isn't drained by the sprinting, it's developed, if and only if it's counterbalanced by the recovery periods.

How do we recover from an illness? Usually, we rest. The busyness of life and leadership is not our ally in our spiritual formation. Richard Foster says that hurry (along with noise and crowds) opposes our spiritual growth.[5] Yet, how often do we create space in our lives, get away from the constant soundtrack in our earbuds, and be quiet? Sometimes we think we're alone, but our phone, iPad, and laptop are at our side so we don't miss anything, and we keep living and leading while others demand our time and attention. Retreats, camps, and short-term trips are such powerful experiences because we're spending time away and giving attention to things that we've long ignored. To gain fresh perspective and listen to the Holy Spirit, we need to do the same personally.

So what can you do? Here's one exercise. (1) Make a three-month calendar. (2) Identify the sprint times that are coming in the next three months. (3) A couple days before and after the sprint times, block out times for spiritual reading, prayer, rest, and recovery. Actually write them on your calendar. And keep them clear of other activities.

MANAGING OUR TIME

Though not all margins are about time, disciplined time management is an important skill for ministry success, and a lack of time management contributes to an inability to be productive in ministry. The following are five time-management practices that you can begin this week. They will help you to be more disciplined and productive, and establish better margins in your life.

1. Work in ninety-minute increments. Some experts think we're wired to work ninety minutes at a time. They recommend starting a timer, work on your project for ninety minutes with no interruptions. Then take a break for at least sixty minutes for other responsibilities or renewal activities. If you gave six hours of your best uninterrupted time each day to your primary work tasks, you would focus more on your work than the average worker gives their work each day.

2. Work in twenty-five-minute increments. If ninety minutes seems ambitious, then try a twenty-five-minute version. Work for twenty-five minutes and then take a five-minute break. Keep doing this throughout the day, and see if it helps.

3. Each week, find two hours to be alone and in silence. No music. Books or a Bible are allowed, as are paper and pen. I recommend no computer or tablet, and definitely no phone. Nothing should be allowed to penetrate the silence. You can do it. The rest of your life will still be there for you after 120 minutes (about the length of a popular movie). Get alone with God. Let him tell you why you are there.

4. Every six weeks, spend a day away in solitude and study. No technology, if possible. If music is helpful, go the first half without it and end with it.

5. Track your time for a week at least once a month. Create a weekly grid with a column for every day and then a row for every thirty minutes from 7 a.m. until 9 p.m. Keep track of how you spend those fourteen hours each day, writing something in every box. Go over it with your supervisor and then make a plan or schedule for the following week that addresses some of the patterns you two noticed.

BURNOUT

Burnout is in the top three topics of concern for ministry leaders. It's mentioned nearly weekly in Christian leadership circles because so many people report experiencing it. We come to the end of our emotions and abilities, and we feel barren, empty, and dusty. I think Parker Palmer's definition of burnout is helpful: "Though usually regarded as the result of trying to give too much, burnout in my experience results from trying to give what I do not possess."[6]

What I do not possess. Think about that in relation to burnout and to margins. We try to fire up our work and offer something to others. But our carafe is nearly empty, and, like a little coffee on the burner over time, we burn, begin to smoke, and stink. What was once full of flavor and aromatic appeal becomes tarry and repugnant. Burnout is the symptom, not the problem. The problems are found along the path toward burnout.

I walked into Pastor Devin's office; he was a former pastor who burned out in ministry. All of his books, papers, mailers, and even his seminary transcripts were untouched; it looked as if he had been in the office the day before. But he had left eighteen months prior. It was a bit spooky. I met with the volunteers; they were fried too, and bitter about the pastor's sudden abandonment even a year and a half later. Devin's path to burnout sounded familiar: isolation from others, inability to learn from others, lack of a mentor, ministering out of an achievement approach versus shepherding, and a personal inability to practice Christ-centered spiritual disciplines. The church had just hired his replacement, so there was hope for better days ahead.

We will grow weary in ministry; it's part of the job. Jesus grew weary. But I think self-sufficiency is the potting soil in which burnout sinks its roots. We've filled ourselves with ourselves, and that won't nurture us for long. Neither will it bear any fruit. We think we can save one more person, leap one taller building, and flex our muscles, and we'll overcome any dry periods. We forget what Jesus demonstrated: ministry is doing the Father's work, not ours.

Jesus regularly turned to his Father for refreshment, recalibration, and rest. And we don't. We neglect the soul in our leadership development and forget that at the core is a leader who needs to grow and develop too. The path out of burnout is not to do more but to rest, renew, and be revived in God, allowing the Spirit to heal and mend. Margins give us space to do that.

MARGINS MATTER

What irritates you about other drivers on the road? Not using a turn signal? Going too slow? Tailgating? Texting while driving? People who honk their horn at you the second the light turns green? I've ridden in cars with men and women who love Jesus and give graciously to the church and missions. But once they're in a car, there's a *big* change. They honk their horns or call other drivers "turkey" or worse.

There's something about the rules of the road and our own desire to get somewhere fast that brings out raw emotion. We feel superior to others on the road. Our travel is more important than the purposes of others on the road. We see other drivers' needs (even to drive safely) and desires (to look at the scenery) as less legitimate than ours.[7] We believe that other drivers are in *our* way. It's irrelevant that they are trying to get somewhere as well. Until we realize that we know the other driver from church!

What if we assume that everyone is trying to drive his or her best? What if we assume that others are equally concerned about many of the same things that agitate us? We could do the same in the rest of life too. What if we begin trusting others more in ministries, businesses, and churches, where mistrust is too common?

While we are pushing to the edge of our margins in time, hurry, noise, and crowds, we bump up against others who are pushing to similar edges. What if we gave some margin to each other? Some of us give more space to people we know than people we don't. Some of us do the opposite. But what if we gave grace-filled, grace-granting margin to those who irritate us, who bless us, who we lead, who we follow, who have loved us and who have hurt us?

It's in the margins where creativity hangs out, where Spirit-led reflection allows us to see blind spots in our spiritual life. It's in the margins where God makes notes on our story. It's where we see that we need to forgive as we're forgiven. It's in the margins where we allow God to grow us in grace toward others and deeper trust in Christ.

FOR GREATER AWARENESS

1. Are you comfortable with the margins in your life? Do you see areas where you might need to make a larger margin to work better and more efficiently?

2. What does establishing margins in your everyday life look like? What do margins on a yearly basis look like for you?

3. What is your plan for making sure that you have spiritual margins? Have you been embarrassed or caught off-guard when asked a question that you should have known the answer to? How can you prevent that as you set up spiritual margins?

4. In our day, social margins can be hard to set. What is your philosophy on your social media usage? Do you have one you can easily articulate to others? Should we have margins on it?

5. The apostle Paul says that we are to redeem time. Go back through the chapter and look at some of the exercises relating to making the most of our time. What changes could you make to be more effective?

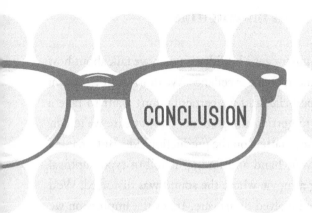

CONCLUSION

I STARTED OUT IN THE MUSIC FIELD supervising a group of roadies that set up Christian concerts in auditoriums. We wore black shirts and understood that duct tape solved most of life's practical problems. We once hired a company who had just worked with a major secular band to run sound for one of our shows. As their crew set up the speakers and microphone stands, they began to measure the distances between various instruments on the stage. The guy became confused in his counting (it was rock and roll, after all) and then stopped. He eyeballed it and said to his partner, "Oh well, close enough for Christian rock."

My crew chuckled nervously. Truthfully, the guy was right; we Christians weren't as concerned about precision as what they were accustomed to in mainstream shows. Some things seemed less important. However, that day's comment has stuck with me for thirty years, because it was about more than where to put a microphone stand, it was about excellence and the perception that Christian music was comfortable with mediocrity.[1]

Those of us in ministry get a bit fidgety when we talk about how to expect, pursue, and manage excellence. We don't want to appear focused on the superficial, and we certainly don't want to take a tyrannical posture to getting things done. I'm not sure we're convinced that excellence matters on the production side. But imagine getting a book in your hand and finding it full of typographical errors, or watching a movie where the sound was distorted. We'd think that someone involved didn't care. That's the impression we can give when we don't pursue our best in ministry.

Amazingly, God has entrusted his message, ministry, and church to us—we play a role in organizing and leading Christian ministry. That certainly creates a performance pressure at times; only mystics would say otherwise. Though most ministry has no actual stage, some days walking out our front door feels like we are walking into the spotlight. What will happen today? What problems will arise that we'll need to solve? Who will need a listening ear at the last minute? How will God lead me today?

We are participants in the mission of God. We can choose to be disobedient, to be legalistic, or to shrink from our responsibilities. We can choose to be overbearing or be like the servant who buried his talents in the ground, either fearful to make a mistake or too lazy to work with what he had been given (Mt 25:14-30). Or we can choose to do the work necessary so we are well-prepared and well-practiced to do our part. Like Paul, we can choose to *press on* to take hold of what Christ has called us to (Phil 3:14).

Press on. *Make it count.* I like that phrase. It serves as a checkpoint for me to do my best toward achieving the end goal. The apostle Paul said something similar, "Whatever you do, work at it with all your heart, as working for the Lord" (Col 3:23). The phrase "all your heart" means to do so willingly, with all of the life, inner self, and distinction as is possible.

Make it count, with all your might and heart.

What can we do now to make the most of our ministry days? Rather, what role should excellence play day-to-day as we focus on the end goal? This book has dealt with a range of blind spots common to young leaders. I want to wrap up this book with some very practical ideas for your ministry leadership. If our desire is to do our best where God has placed us, then these are meant to encourage you to run your best.

Be enthused. Enthusiasm is not extroversion; nor is it being excited. It is demonstrated confidence for what one believes and does. We often call it "passion." The biblical word is translated as "zeal" or "single-minded desire."[2] It's interesting that there's a relationship between enthusiasm and devotion, isn't it?

Some denominational traditions are skeptical of celebration and joy. We think holy and worshiping people have to look like they're in pain or discomfort. I've seen many worship music leaders (and I am one) who seem unhappy as they lead. Though we're comfortable with adults demonstrating exuberance for their sports team, even dressing in costumes, we are suspicious of people who are joyful about God.

I once got a call from a man who wanted to be an intern in the ministry I led. He said he wanted to be my shadow and learn how to speak, teach, and lead upfront. But problems emerged immediately. Every time I handed him the microphone, he shrank back, figuratively and literally. His head dropped, he stepped back from the group, and his tone lacked conviction. I tried to work with him, and each week he said, "Yeah, yeah, I've got it now," and the following week his stage presence was lackadaisical. When he began to speak, the teenagers lost interest almost immediately, and I eventually had to put him in a different ministry role.

Like it or not, a dynamic, positive, upbeat presence communicates conviction, and it reflects the presence of God within us. In fact, persuasion research shows we think someone is more credible the more they show enthusiasm. This effect is the reason that infomercial hosts are loud and expressive or why politicians walk on stage with a big smile, happy waves, and even clapping with the audience. Enthusiasm stimulates people to listen.

Enthusiasm is more than just personality. I've seen even the most introverted people find how to express themselves and connect well with others in life-changing ways. Certainly, we don't want to be misguided in our enthusiasm, but even that line of thinking shows we don't know what genuine enthusiasm is. Our enthusiasm flows out of our joyful confidence in Jesus Christ and the work of the Holy Spirit. If we aren't drawing deeply from God, then all of it is a veneer. Perhaps these five elements of true enthusiasm will help:

1. *We are convinced.* Enthusiasm is not volume, it's conviction. We are drawn to those who are convinced. Without conviction, enthusiasm can become manipulation or intimidation.

2. *We are prepared.* Preparation means we have spent time developing, reviewing, and revising the material. Perhaps no other habitual practice separates productive leaders from the rest.

3. *We engage others.* Enthusiasm assumes genuine interest in others. When there's little attention given to those we lead, enthusiasm becomes self-serving.

4. *We are positive.* We're committed to helping people take their best next steps. True enthusiasm stands alone in a world too used to criticism and negativity.

5. *We stay fresh.* We are fresh when we're staying spiritually vibrant, physically fit, and mentally healthy. Where there's a lack of enthusiasm, weariness isn't far behind.

Develop endurance. Christian ministry resembles a long-term investment more than a pawnshop transaction. We aren't letting people hold something valuable in exchange for just a little of our time or attention. We are putting smaller bits of attention into them regularly over a long time.

The economy of people work isn't built around one-shot chances (like a lottery), but in two significant ways it's built on the principle of compounding interest. First, small things over time add up to something valuable. Second, ministry's effect is usually best calculated in the future rather than in the moment. Sometimes what seems to have gone wrong, God will use in dramatic ways.

Andrew Root, author and professor at Luther Seminary in St. Paul, has championed endurance's role in a Christ-centered theology of incarnational (relational) ministry. Our presence in others' lives is not message dependent or veiled in a way to control or manipulate others into doing what we want them to do. Instead, we offer godly teaching, counsel, and faithful presence in others' lives. We share with them in joy, suffering, and life, and for the long haul, regardless of their response to our message. Root says our relationships are to be unconditional, agenda free, and Christian.[3]

Endurance stands in marked contrast to today's "I quit" culture, which says that if you don't like something you can just quit. If the job is too tough, just quit. If you don't like a coach, just quit the team. If you aren't fulfilled in your marriage, just quit. If your pastor says something you don't like, you can attend another church or just quit going at all. If no one is

> Incarnational ministry has no easy "I quit" button to push.

responding the way you want in the work that God gave you, quit.

Mary Beth has been counseling with Laurie for over twenty-three years. When the two met, Laurie really shouldn't have been alive given all of the abuse and lifestyle choices she had experienced. Their relationship has gone through its share of ups and downs. There have been multiple periods of prodigal exploration to every imaginable extreme, sudden starts and stops marked by long periods of Laurie's silence and anger. Mary Beth just modeled an "I'm not going anywhere" attitude, having gone through other "don't talk to me" periods with Laurie before.

Some Christians, churches, and ministries gave up on Laurie along the way; she certainly made it difficult, turning on the people who love her the most. The churches didn't know what to do with someone who couldn't clean up within six months and who had more than a few very public failures within the small community. Those cause embarrassment and frustration for churches, ministerial staff, and Mary Beth. But Mary Beth and her family aren't going anywhere, because Jesus didn't quit; even to the very end he forgave.

Over two decades of presence and prayer may be what it takes for someone to experience Christ's forgiveness and redemption, which Laurie has. The spiritual growth in Laurie over the last two years has been remarkable, and she's found a church that provides the needed support for her to take healthy steps, even though it sometimes feels like three steps forward and two steps back. Laurie will make it, but it won't be easy for her or for those who work with her.

Here's a secret about long-term ministry: there will be periods of discouragement, sometimes *long* periods. Eugene Peterson described them as "the Badlands" like the desolate rocky area in South Dakota.[4] One period may last for years. Don't give in too fast or give up too soon, unless God makes it clear that it's time. There are times, of course, when you will need to move on, but you have to be very sure, because quitting when it gets tough or when facing opposition (or even rejection!) is not biblical. It's more cultural. Whether it's volunteering at a church, serving on a university campus, or on a church staff, your long-term presence and persistence may have a fruitful season ahead, one beyond your imagination, if you stay and continue to till the soil. In ministry we usually expect way too much change in one year, and way too little in four.[5]

Express empathy. If there ever was a golden ticket (à la Willy Wonka) to get inside the "guarded fence" of other people's lives, it would be empathy, our capacity to look at life from the other person's perspective. When I watch people who connect well with others, empathy is always present.

Have you connected so deeply with someone that you knew they understood the real you? Maybe it was a coach, teacher, pastor, or one of your family members. When you were facing the pain of a lost animal, that person was quick to say, "I bet that hurts. That dog listened to you when no one else would, right?" They listened carefully to your heart, looked for clues about your connection, and shared the pain before they offered cures.

The apostle John describes Jesus' empathy this way: "He did not need any testimony about mankind, for he knew what was in each person" (Jn 2:25). And later, when Mary was weeping near Lazarus's grave, Jesus wept (Jn 11:35). Clearly, Jesus was capable of giving Lazarus life. But he also was capable of empathizing with Mary's loss, and joined her in her grief.

Those who connect well with us understand and can relate such in a way that we want to be with them. If I gave you one skill to learn that will have an immediate and positive effect on your ministry and life, it's this. Empathy connects us with others; it's often described as "sharing our hearts." It starts with prayerful listening before you speak, and hearing questions before you give answers.

Enthusiasm and empathy give life and breath to ministry. Their opposites deflate relationships and community.

Effective teaching. You have probably heard this question: If a tree falls in the woods and no one is around to hear it, does it make a sound? I ask a similar one: If a teacher teaches in a woods and no one is around to hear it, does learning take place? Well, of course not, we would say. Yet sometimes the evaluation of teaching and events happens as if the presence and participation of learners didn't matter. We analyze the presentation, the media and music, and remember the illustrations we used. We may even talk about how attentive the audience seemed as we talked. But the criteria for effectiveness should have little to do with how smooth the technology or transitions went. The evaluation should focus on the learning that took place, of the changes in the thinking and lives of the learners. We measure effectiveness by the learners' growth.

Think about the teaching sessions and events that led to lasting change in your own life. Think about the teacher who changed your approach to God, the small group leader who consistently challenged you to follow God's lead. What did they do? How did they make the sessions point toward deep engagement with the pain of the world and the power of God? Think about the conference where every program element was so well crafted that no one was confused, and God grabbed ahold of lives. Apply what they did to your own teaching.

Have an engaging style. There is a new reality for ministry leaders in our interactive, open-source world. The days of participation out of obligation have faded. People only show up to things that are meaningful to their lives. So something other than duty or gaining information prompts people to show up. People pay attention to what is *meaningful*, to what helps them grow and live better tomorrow than they did yesterday. We share the divine answer to that quest, usually from the middle of a community of fellow seekers.

Almost everyone I know who is successful in ministry is engaging in some way. Some are engaging in front of large groups. Others are engaging because they listen and understand well in small groups. Engaging means that we connect in ways *that are meaningful to others*. Think about the people who chose to be around Jesus. Luke tells us that "the tax collectors and sinners were all gathering around to hear Jesus" (Lk 15:1). Mark says that "many tax collectors and sinners were eating with him and his disciples" because "there were many who followed him" (Mk 2:15). It wasn't because Jesus was letting them off the hook. But Jesus engaged with and valued the people who came to him, and they responded to his message.

Encourage others in their faith. We often think of encouragement as affirmation. But what if we saw it more like giving hope as we encourage others to persevere, to continue on? A frequent command of Jesus was "fear not." Some might think it would have been "repent" or "obey," but Jesus knew that fear is a debilitating problem. In the middle of fear, experiencing hope through encouragement gives strength to continue. Giving hope is what effective leaders do.

Jesus did this with his disciples at the Last Supper. He encouraged them, "Peace I leave with you; my peace I give you. I do not give to you as the world gives. Do not let your hearts be troubled and do not be afraid" (Jn 14:27). If you want to make a difference in the spiritual lives of others, cheer them on to keep running the race, to not be afraid, and to trust in Jesus as they follow him.

ALL THE WAY TO THE FINISH LINE!

When I started developing this book, I wanted it to be an encouragement, to not have a negative tone, and to help us develop greater awareness without taking the focus off of Jesus. In the last few months, as I've wrapped up my writing, God has worked with me on two topics from this book. Ministry's race is long and, though it may be going well, I've discovered that reviewing this book regularly has helped me discover where I've gotten off course.

The older I get, the more I see that a fundamental goal to our Christian work is to draw close in intimacy and loving obedience to Jesus and to help others do the same. I love the hymn "All the Way My Savior Leads Me." Its words have been constant reminders of the ultimate goal for each day along ministry's journey. At the end of my days I want to be able to look back and say with confidence, "This my song through endless ages: / Jesus led me all the way."[6]

The Coach of coaches will run alongside us at times, cheering us along each winding path, working to keep us from straying. It's up to us to respond to his guidance and be in our best shape so we can hear and heed his voice.

May you run the race of ministry to the finish line in great faithfulness, vigilant and attentive to blind spots that work to impede faithfulness and effectiveness. And may God do his creative and fruitful work through you wherever he leads you and in whatever capacity he places you.

This book was written in community with friends and colleagues who molded it over time; the fingerprints of each can be found all over it. I am forever indebted to Helen Lee for her vision, editorial expertise, and gracious encouragement. Her own experience as a ministry leader and mentor gave her editorial work depth and practicality beyond mere wordsmithing. National ministry leader and friend Jason Jensen graciously gave attention to every sentence, offering his usual astute advice and gentle guidance. My friend and author Jon Swanson (300wordsaday.com) helped me with the last edit, a blessing of pastoral wisdom and practical insight. Drew Blankman provided helpful editorial feedback along the way and then, when Helen was promoted at IVP, ably stepped in to pilot the final stages of the publishing process. I'm grateful to all four of these people for their direction throughout the book's development.

This book wouldn't exist without the timely and professional encouragement of Holly Root (Root Literary), shrewd advice from Rick Lawrence (Group

Publishing), and the vision of David Zimmerman, who first took on the project for InterVarsity Press. Each understood the goal of this book, helped shape its direction, and encouraged me in moments when I was about to give up.

I am grateful to the following for their guidance and input: Steve Laube, Ginny Olson, Jama Davis, Kathy Belcher, and David McCabe. Jon Swanson has become a close colleague and friend over the last two years, and I'm thankful for his encouragement and editorial help in the revision process.

I also need to acknowledge the exemplary Christian workers who shaped my life and gave me solid footing for a life in ministry leadership: Miss Miller, Patti DeVore, Bill Weberling, Ken Vance, Chuck Swindoll, Dave Schramm, Bob Laurent, Jay Kesler, Lynn Ziegenfuss, Dave Rahn, Tim Atkins, Tom Clounie, Gary Aupperle, Matt Hartsell, Dave Engbrecht, Eugene Carpenter, and Norman Bridges. My life is partly a product of their collective investment, and for that I am indebted.

I am fortunate to work and teach in a vibrant community of exceptional faculty, staff, and students at Bethel College (bethel college.edu) under the leadership of President Gregg Chenoweth and Dr. Barb Bellefeuille.

I owe much more than I realize to my parents, Rev. Dale and Marian Linhart, an exemplary pastoral couple whose lives, words, and prayers continue to shape me in profound ways. I learned my first lessons in Christian theology and pastoral leadership sitting on the back patio swing with my dad, and I learned about the educator's life from my stepmom.

Finally, I am grateful to the one with whom I've shared many ministry moments and life-changing conversations, Kelly, my best friend and the love of my life. Her commitment to following Jesus, patience with my ups and downs, and encouragement to persevere in the midst of difficult circumstances have been steadfast. My three adult children, Lauren, Jayson, and Sean, continue to capture my heart each year in new ways as I watch them learn and mature. I'm a proud husband and father.

NOTES

INTRODUCTION

[1]Mark DeVries, *Sustainable Youth Ministry* (Downers Grove, IL: InterVarsity Press, 2008), 6.

[2]John Calvin, *Institutes of the Christian Religion* 1.1.1, ed. J. T. Neill, Library of Christian Classics (Louisville, KY: Westminster Press, 1960).

[3]Timothy Keller, *Prayer: Experiencing Awe and Intimacy with God* (New York: Dutton, 2015), 135.

[4]Arbinger Institute, *Leadership and Self-Deception: Getting Out of the Box* (San Francisco: Berrett-Koehler, 2002), 15.

[5]Gordon T. Smith, *Voice of Jesus: Discernment, Prayer and the Witness of the Spirit* (Downers Grove, IL: InterVarsity Press, 2003), 33.

[6]Ibid., 64.

[7]David G. Benner, *The Gift of Being Yourself: The Sacred Call to Self-Discovery* (Downers Grove, IL: InterVarsity Press, 2004), 63.

1 SEEING THE RACE BEFORE US

[1]Tim Elmore, *Habitudes* (Norcross: GA: Growing Leaders, 2004), i. Dr. Elmore has written a series of helpful *Habitude* booklets published by Growing Leaders, Inc.

[2]Henri Nouwen, *In the Name of Jesus: Reflections on Christian Leadership* (New York: Crossroad, 1989), 10.

[3]See Craig S. Keener, *The IVP Bible Background Commentary: New Testament* (Downers Grove, IL: IVP Academic, 1993), 623.

[4]In Ephesians 4:20–5:4 Paul also describes the process as "putting off the old self," to be made new in our minds, and to then put on the new self—a helpful description of the redemptive process of reflection.

[5]Parker Palmer, *Let Your Life Speak: Listening for the Voice of Vocation* (San Francisco: Jossey-Bass, 1999), 30.

[6] J. Luft and H. Ingham, "The Johari Window: A Graphic Model of Interpersonal Awareness," proceedings of the Western Training: Laboratory in Group Development, University of California Los Angeles, 1955.

[7] I first heard Rick Lawrence, author and editor of *Group* magazine, say this at the AYME Conference in Washington, DC, October 2014.

[8] See Skye Jethani, *With: Reimagining the Way You Relate to God* (Nashville: Thomas Nelson, 2011), 11.

2 SEEING YOUR SELF

[1] I am grateful to Jon for his editorial help, pastoral wisdom, and biblical examples. You can connect with Jon at www.300wordsaday.com or check out his many books on Amazon.

[2] Søren Kierkegaard, *Either/Or*, vols. 1-2, trans. and ed. Howard V. Hong and Edna H. Hong (Princeton, NJ: Princeton University Press, 1987); Thomas Merton, *New Seeds of Contemplation* (New York: New Directions, 1972).

[3] Thomas Merton, *Thoughts in Solitude* (New York: Farrar, Straus & Giroux, 1999), 18.

[4] Robert Mulholland Jr., *Invitation to a Journey: A Road Map for Spiritual Formation* (Downers Grove, IL: InterVarsity Press, 1993), 27.

[5] David G. Benner, *The Gift of Being Yourself: The Sacred Call to Self-Discovery* (Downers Grove, IL: InterVarsity Press, 2004), 78.

[6] Ibid., 76.

[7] South African pastor and author Mark Tittley gets the credit for giving me this analogy after a seminar I led in Johannesburg.

[8] David Grant, personal conversation with the author at Ministry Council meeting of the National Network of Youth Ministries, 2013. You can connect with David at www.twitter.com/david_grant.

[9] Jason Jensen, email communication with the author, October 2015.

[10] This image comes from Stephen Covey, Roger Merrill, and Rebecca Merrill, *First Things First* (New York: Simon & Schuster, 1994).

3 SEEING YOUR PAST

[1] Meg Greenfield, *Washington* (Washington, DC: Public Affairs, 2002).

[2] Laurence Steinberg, *Age of Opportunity: Lessons from the New Science of Adolescence* (New York: Mariner Books, 2015).

[3] Henri Nouwen, *In the Name of Jesus: Reflections on Christian Leadership* (New York: Crossroad, 1989).

[4]Parker Palmer, *Let Your Life Speak: Listening for the Voice of Vocation* (San Francisco: Jossey-Bass, 2000).

4 SEEING YOUR TEMPTATIONS

[1]Ian Morgan Cron and Suzanne Stabile, *The Road Back to You: An Enneagram Journey to Self-Discovery* (Downers Grove, IL: InterVarsity Press, 2016).

[2]Gordon T. Smith, *Voice of Jesus: Discernment, Prayer and the Witness of the Spirit* (Downers Grove, IL: InterVarsity Press, 2003), 41.

[3]Parker Palmer, *The Active Life: A Spirituality of Work, Creativity, and Caring* (San Francisco: Jossey-Bass, 1999), 109.

[4]Mike Myatt, *Hacking Leadership: The Eleven Gaps Every Business Needs to Close and the Secrets to Closing Them Quickly* (Hoboken, NJ: Wiley, 2013), 5.

[5]Leaf Van Boven, "Experientialism, Materialism, and the Pursuit of Happiness," *Review of General Psychology* 9, no. 2 (2005): 132-42.

[6]Diana Garland, "Clergy Sexual Misconduct: Don't Call It an Affair," *Journal of Family and Community Ministries* 26 (2013): 66-96.

[7]For computer accountability, Covenant Eyes software (covenanteyes.com) and Blazing Grace (blazinggrace.org) are helpful resources.

[8]Debra Fileta, "Five Things We Can Learn from the Ashley Madison Scandal," *Relevant*, August 24, 2015, www.relevantmagazine.com/current/5 -things-we-can-learn-ashley-madison-scandal.

[9]"Stats," *XXXChurch*, accessed June 6, 2016, www.xxxchurch.com/stats.

[10]Joe Stowell, *Redefining Leadership: Character-Driven Habits of Effective Leaders* (Grand Rapids: Zondervan, 2014), 59.

5 SEEING YOUR EMOTIONS

[1]Gordon T. Smith, *Voice of Jesus: Discernment, Prayer and the Witness of the Spirit* (Downers Grove, IL: InterVarsity Press, 2003), 65.

[2]Ibid., 39.

[3]Thanks to Jason Jensen, national field director of InterVarsity Christian Fellowship, for this quote.

[4]Kary Oberbrunner, *The Deeper Path* (Grand Rapids: Baker, 2014), 121-25.

[5]Ibid, 124.

[6]J. Oswald Sanders, *Spiritual Leadership: Principles of Excellence for Every Believer* (Chicago: Moody Publishers, 2007).

[7]The story can be found at Hitendra Wadhwa, "The Wrath of a Great Leader," *Inc.*, updated January 21, 2013, www.inc.com/hitendra-wadhwa /great-leadership-how-martin-luther-king-jr-wrestled-with-anger.html.

6 SEEING YOUR PRESSURES

[1]This book doesn't allow adequate space to deal with these topics in any depth. One of my most used tools for understanding our personality and preferences is the MCore Motivational Blueprint (motivationalcore.com). And Tom Rath's *Strengths Finder 2.0* (Washington, DC: Gallup Press, 2007) has been a bestseller for years because it has helped many discover their strongest capacities.

7 SEEING YOUR CONFLICTS

[1]From Dave Engbrecht, pastor of Nappanee Missionary Church.

[2]I learned the helpful concept of "coupons" from author, speaker, and former president of Youth for Christ and of Taylor University, Jay Kesler.

[3]Bob Goff, *Love Does* (Nashville: Thomas Nelson, 2012), 204.

[4]Signe Whitson, "Seven Reasons Why People Use Passive Aggressive Behavior," *Psychology Today*, March 16, 2014, www.psychologytoday.com/blog /passive-aggressive-diaries/201403/7-reasons-why-people-use-passive-aggressive-behavior.

[5]Ronald Koteskey and Bonnie Koteskey, "Missionary Care: Resources for Missions and Mental Health," *Missionary Care*, http://missionarycare.com /passive-aggressive-behavior.html.

[6]Some of the material in this section comes from Muriel Maignan Wilkins, "Signs You're Being Passive-Aggressive," *Harvard Business Review*, June 20, 2014, https://hbr.org/2014/06/signs-youre-being-passive-aggressive.

[7]David Livermore's must-read book *Cultural Intelligence: Improving Your CQ to Engage Our Multicultural World* (Grand Rapids: Baker Academic, 2009) will help clarify cultural differences regarding communication, conflict, and many more areas.

8 SEEING YOUR MARGINS

[1]Jon Swanson, *A Great Work: A Conversation with Nehemiah for People Who Are Doing Great Works* (Fort Wayne, IN: Createspace, 2013).

[2]Jon Swanson, "Morning Coffee," *300 Words a Day*, May 8, 2013, https://300wordsaday.com/?s=morning+coffee.

[3]Bill Hybels, *Axiom: Powerful Leadership Proverbs* (Grand Rapids: Zondervan, 2008), 197.

[4]Pamela Slim, *Body of Work* (New York: Penguin, 2013), 7.

[5]Richard Foster, *Celebration of Discipline: The Path to Spiritual Growth* (San Francisco: HarperSanFrancisco, 2002).

[6]Parker Palmer, *Let Your Life Speak: Listening for the Voice of Vocation* (San Francisco: Jossey-Bass, 1999), 49.

[7]Arbinger Institute, *Leadership and Self-Deception: Getting Out of the Box* (San Francisco: Berrett-Koehler, 2002), 34.

CONCLUSION

[1]This idea is neither new nor mine alone. For more, see Franky Schaeffer, *Addicted to Mediocrity* (New Orleans: Cornerstone Books, 1981).

[2]M. H. Manser, *Dictionary of Bible Themes* (London: Martin Manser, 2009).

[3]Andrew Root, *Revisiting Relational Youth Ministry: From a Strategy of Influence to a Theology of Incarnation* (Downers Grove, IL: InterVarsity Press, 2007).

[4]Eugene Peterson, *The Pastor: A Memoir* (New York: HarperOne, 2011), 207.

[5]Jason Jensen shared this in his review of this book.

[6]Fanny Crosby, "All the Way My Savior Leads Me," 1875.

PRAXIS
EQUIPPING LEADERS FOR MINISTRY

"...TO EQUIP HIS PEOPLE FOR WORKS OF SERVICE,

SO THAT THE BODY OF CHRIST MAY BE BUILT UP."

EPHESIANS 4:12

God has called us to ministry. But it's not enough to have a vision for ministry if you don't have the practical skills for it. Nor is it enough to do the work of ministry if what you do is headed in the wrong direction. We need both vision *and* expertise for effective ministry. We need *praxis*.

Praxis puts theory into practice. It brings cutting-edge ministry expertise from visionary practitioners. You'll find sound biblical and theological foundations for ministry in the real world, with concrete examples for effective action and pastoral ministry. Praxis books are more than the "how to"—they're also the "why to." And because *being* is every bit as important as *doing*, Praxis attends to the inner life of the leader as well as the outer work of ministry. Feed your soul, and feed your ministry.

If you are called to ministry, you know you can't do it on your own. Let Praxis provide the companions you need to equip God's people for life in the kingdom.

www.ivpress.com/praxis